THE SIMPLE 5-INGREDIENT ANTI-INFLAMMATORY COOKBOOK

100+ EASY RECIPES FOR BUSY PEOPLE TO HEAL INFLAMMATION & BOOST IMMUNITY

DOLORES ABRAMS

© Copyright 2024 Dolores Abrams. All rights reserved.

The content contained within this book may not be reproduced, duplicated, or transmitted without direct written permission from the author or the publisher. Under no circumstances will any blame or legal responsibility be held against the publisher or author for any damages, reparation, or monetary loss due to the information contained within this book, either directly or indirectly.

Legal Notice:

This book is copyright protected. It is only for personal use. You cannot amend, distribute, sell, use, quote, or paraphrase any part of the content within this book without the consent of the author or publisher.

Disclaimer Notice:

Please note that the information contained within this document is for educational and entertainment purposes only. All efforts have been executed to present accurate, up-to-date, reliable, and complete information. No warranties of any kind are declared or implied. Readers acknowledge that the author is not engaged in the rendering of legal, financial, medical, or professional advice. The content within this book has been derived from various sources. Please consult a licensed professional before attempting any techniques outlined in this book.

By reading this document, the reader agrees that under no circumstances is the author responsible for any losses, direct or indirect, that are incurred as a result of the use of the information contained within this document, including, but not limited to, errors, omissions, or inaccuracies.

Contents

Introduction 7
Anti-Inflammatory Diet 8
The Problem with Inflammation 9
Why 5 Ingredients Are All You Need 9
Understanding Anti-Inflammatory Eating................................... 10

Breakfast 12
Turmeric Spiced Smoothie Bowl.. 13
Avocado and Spainach Omelet 14
Sweet Potato and Kale Hash with Poached Egg 15
Anti-Inflammatory Golden Milk Oats 16
Green Apple and Almond Butter Toast.. 17
Quinoa Breakfast Bowl with Almonds 18
Banana and Walnut Chia Pudding 19
Coconut Yogurt with Berries and Seeds 20
Lemon Turmeric Overnight Oats 21
Sweet Potato Pancakes with Cinnamon 22
Apple and Almond Butter Wrap 23
Turmeric and Ginger Infused Porridge 24
Avocado and Tomato Whole Grain Toast 25
Spiced Pear and Oat Parfait 26
Spinach and Mushroom Egg Muffins 27
Mango and Coconut Chia Pudding 28
Lemon and Flaxseed Protein Pancakes 29
Matcha Green Tea Smoothie 30
Golden Milk Breakfast Bowl...31
Raspberry and Almond Oatmeal 32
Ginger and Apple Spiced Smoothie 33
Turmeric Scrambled Eggs with Spinach......................................34
Roasted Sweet Potato and Avocado Mash 35
Greek-Inspired Egg Wraps 36
Cinnamon and Pumpkin Breakfast Porridge 37

Lunch 38
Grilled Salmon with Quinoa and Spinach 39
Roasted Vegetable and Chickpea Bowl 40
Turkey and Avocado Lettuce Wraps 41
Chicken Salad with Olive Oil Dressing 42
Spicy Quinoa Salad with Kale and Nuts 43
Grilled Chicken with Zucchini Noodles 44
Avocado and Cucumber Sushi Rolls 45
Sweet Potato and Lentil Curry 46
Salmon and Cucumber Salad 47
Turmeric Chickpea Buddha Bowl 48
Baked Falafel with Tahini Drizzle 49
Warm Beet and Spinach Salad 50
Tomato and Avocado Gazpacho 51
Lemon Herb Shrimp Salad 52
Cauliflower Rice Stir-Fry with Tofu 53
Coconut Curry Lentil Soup 54
Roasted Squash and Quinoa Salad 55
Grilled Eggplant and Chickpea Wraps 56
Ginger Lime Shrimp Bowls 57
Grilled Turkey Patties with Cucumber Salad 58
Steamed Veggie with Sesame Dressing 59
Spicy Lentil and Tomato Soup 60
Zucchini and Sweet Potato Fritters 61
Ginger Chicken and Brown Rice Bowl 62
Roasted Veggie Wraps with Hummus 63

Dinner 64
Baked Cod with Tomato and Basil Sauce 65
Ginger Sesame Shrimp Stir-Fry with Zucchini 66
Turmeric-spiced roasted Cauliflower and Tofu 67
Salmon with Dill and Lemon Sauce 68
Cauliflower and Chickpea Stew 69
Lentil Curry with Sweet Potatoes 70
Seared Scallops with Garlic and Spinach 71

Turmeric Chicken Stir-Fry with Veggies 72
Baked Eggplant with Tomato Sauce 73
Spinach and Mushroom Stuffed Bell Peppers 74
Roasted Zucchini and Quinoa Bowl 75
Miso-Glazed Salmon with Bok Choy 76
Sweet Potato and Kale Stew 77
Butternut Squash Soup with Coconut Milk 78
Lemon Thyme Chicken with Roasted Vegetables..79
Garlic Ginger Shrimp with Green Beans..80
Zucchini Noodles with Pesto and Cherry Tomatoes...................................81
Baked Trout with Dill and Lemon...82
Roasted Cauliflower Steaks with Turmeric Sauce 83
Coconut Curry Shrimp with Spinach 84
Grilled Turkey Burgers with Avocado Salsa 85
Spaghetti Squash with Basil and Garlic 86
Baked Chicken Thighs with Kale and Sweet Potatoeas 87
Lentil Stew with Garlic and Rosemary..88
Roasted Brussels Sprouts and Chickpea Bowl..89

Snacks 90
Cucumber Slices with Turmeric Hummus 91
Mixed Berry and Walnut Energy Bites..92
Carrot Sticks with Lemon Tahini Dip 93
Coconut and Matcha Bliss Balls 94
Dark Chocolate Dipped Strawberries 95
Sliced Pear with Walnut and Honey Drizzle 96
Pumpkin Seeds with Chili Powder 97
Avocado and Tomato Mini Toasts..98
Mango and Almond Butter Roll-Ups 99
Baked Zucchini Chips 100
Cucumber and Dill Yogurt Dip 101
Sweet Potato Rounds with Hummus...102
Fresh Pineapple with Coconut Flakes...103
Raw Veggie Sticks with Cashew Dip..104

Cinnamon Roasted Apples 105
Desserts 106
Dark Chocolate Avocado Mousse 107
Raspberry and Almond Flour Crumble 108
Matcha Green Tea Coconut Balls 109
Anti-Inflammatory Turmeric Latte Ice Cream 110
Lemon and Blueberry Coconut Tart 111
Sweet Potato Brownies 112
Orange and Ginger Sorbet 113
Banana and Turmeric Ice Cream 114
Ginger and Lemon Cake Bites 115
Pumpkin and Coconut Cream Mousse 116

30 Days Meal Plan 117
1st Week Meal Plan 119
2nd Week Meal Plan 120
3rd Week Meal Plan 121
4th Week Meal Plan 122
Conclusion 123

INTRODUCTION

Inflammation is the body's natural way of protecting and healing itself, but when it becomes chronic, it can lead to a host of health issues—fatigue, joint pain, digestive discomfort, and even serious conditions like heart disease and diabetes. The good news? You have the power to control and reduce inflammation through the food you eat.

Welcome to The Simple 5-Ingredient Anti-Inflammatory Cookbook, your ultimate guide to eating clean, simple, and healing meals without the stress of complicated recipes or long ingredient lists.

Why Simplicity Matters
In today's fast-paced world, finding time to cook healthy meals can feel impossible. Long shopping lists, elaborate recipes, and unfamiliar ingredients often discourage us from making better food choices. That's where this cookbook comes in.
This book is built on one core principle: simple food is powerful food. Each recipe requires just 5 main ingredients (plus salt and pepper), saving you time, energy, and money. You'll learn how to create delicious, nourishing meals that fight inflammation and boost your immunity—all without overcomplicating your life.

What You'll Find in This Book
This isn't just a cookbook—it's a roadmap to better health. Inside, you'll discover:
- 100+ Easy Recipes: Wholesome meals for breakfast, lunch, dinner, snacks, and even desserts, all using just 5 key ingredients.
- The Basics of Anti-Inflammatory Eating: Learn which foods to embrace, which to limit, and how they impact your body.
- Practical Tips: Simplify meal prep, stock your pantry, and make anti-inflammatory eating part of your everyday life.
- Results You'll Notice Quickly: Reduced bloating, better energy, improved skin, and less joint pain are just the beginning.

Who This Book Is For
Whether you're someone managing a chronic condition, looking to boost your immunity, or simply seeking healthier eating habits, this cookbook is for you. It's designed for anyone who:
- Feels overwhelmed by complex diets.
- Wants quick, easy, and nutritious meals.
- Values flavor, simplicity, and health.

The Power of Five
Why 5 ingredients? Because healing your body doesn't require an endless list of components. With a few high-quality, anti-inflammatory staples, you can create meals that are as effective as they are delicious. By focusing on minimalism, you'll feel empowered, not exhausted.

A Journey to Better Health
This book isn't about restrictive dieting—it's about abundance. You'll discover a variety of meals and flavors that nourish your body and delight your taste buds. Along the way, you'll experience the benefits of anti-inflammatory eating firsthand: reduced pain, better digestion, and improved overall wellness.
So, let's simplify your kitchen, supercharge your meals, and take the first step toward a healthier, more vibrant you. It's time to heal, one 5-ingredient recipe at a time.

ANTI-INFLAMMATORY DIET

Inflammation is a word that's been buzzing around in health conversations for years. At first glance, it might seem like something to avoid entirely. But in reality, inflammation is a natural process—your body's defense mechanism to heal and protect itself. It's what happens when you cut your finger or catch a cold. Acute inflammation helps you recover.

However, chronic inflammation is another story. When inflammation lingers, it can wreak havoc on your body, contributing to conditions such as heart disease, arthritis, diabetes, and even mental health challenges. The good news is that the foods we eat have the power to either fuel this inflammation or fight it.
This book is here to make the latter simple, practical, and delicious.

The Need for Simplicity

Let's face it: life is busy. Between work, family, and other commitments, finding time to research ingredients, plan meals, and prepare elaborate dishes can feel impossible. That's why this cookbook was designed with one simple concept in mind—every recipe uses just 5 main ingredients (plus salt and pepper). You'll be amazed at how much flavor and variety you can achieve with so few components.

By focusing on simplicity, you'll find that eating anti-inflammatory meals becomes less of a chore and more of a joyful habit. Whether you're looking to reduce joint pain, improve digestion, or simply feel better, this approach allows you to achieve your goals without added stress.

The Overwhelming World of Anti-Inflammatory Diets

The world of health and wellness can be overwhelming. One moment, you're told to cut carbs. The next, you're encouraged to focus on whole grains. The conflicting advice is enough to make anyone's head spin. Add in long ingredient lists and complex recipes, and it's no wonder so many people give up before they even start.

But what if it didn't have to be that way? What if you could embrace an anti-inflammatory lifestyle without spending hours in the kitchen or breaking the bank on specialty items? That's the promise of this book: straightforward, accessible, and achievable anti-inflammatory eating.

WHY 5 INGREDIENTS ARE ALL YOU NEED

Think of this cookbook as your tool for turning down the noise. With just 5 ingredients in each recipe, you'll rediscover the joy of cooking while nourishing your body with meals that heal. Each ingredient is carefully selected to maximize anti-inflammatory benefits and create flavors you'll savor.

Simplicity doesn't mean sacrifice. Instead, it allows you to focus on the essentials—real food, real flavor, and real results. You don't need a cupboard full of exotic spices or specialty products to achieve wellness. All you need is a handful of high-quality ingredients and the willingness to try.

THE PROBLEM WITH INFLAMMATION

Inflammation is your body's natural defense mechanism—a process designed to protect and heal. When you scrape your knee, catch a cold, or fight off an infection, inflammation steps in as your body's first responder. In these cases, inflammation is temporary and beneficial, helping you recover.

But what happens when inflammation doesn't go away? That's when it becomes a problem.

Acute vs. Chronic Inflammation
Acute Inflammation
Acute inflammation is short-term and occurs as a response to injury or illness. Symptoms include redness, swelling, pain, or heat, and these usually subside once your body has healed.

Chronic Inflammation
Chronic inflammation, on the other hand, lingers silently. Instead of resolving, it persists for weeks, months, or even years, and this prolonged state can damage tissues and organs. Unlike acute inflammation, chronic inflammation often doesn't present obvious symptoms at first, making it difficult to detect.
What Causes Chronic Inflammation?
Chronic inflammation can be triggered by a variety of factors:
Dietary Choices: Excessive sugar, trans fats, refined carbs, and processed foods can lead to ongoing inflammation.
Stress and Sleep Deprivation: Constant stress and poor-quality sleep can disrupt your body's ability to heal and regulate itself.
Environmental Factors: Exposure to pollutants and toxins in the air, water, and even household products.
Lifestyle Habits: Smoking, excessive alcohol consumption, and lack of exercise exacerbate inflammation.

UNDERSTANDING ANTI-INFLAMMATORY EATING

Inflammation doesn't happen by chance. It's a response triggered by what you put in your body and how you treat it. The foods you eat can either fuel the fire of chronic inflammation or act as a powerful extinguisher. Understanding the connection between diet and inflammation is the first step to reclaiming your health.

What Causes Inflammation?

Inflammation is your immune system's way of protecting you, but when it's constantly activated, it can become harmful. Here are the main culprits behind chronic inflammation:

Refined Sugars and Carbohydrates
Foods high in sugar and refined carbs, like candy, pastries, and white bread, cause rapid spikes in blood sugar, triggering inflammatory responses.
Unhealthy Fats
Trans fats found in processed snacks and fast food, as well as excessive omega-6 fatty acids from refined oils, disrupt the body's natural balance, promoting inflammation.
Processed Foods
Additives, preservatives, and artificial ingredients in packaged foods can stress your body, leading to chronic inflammation over time.
Lifestyle Factors
Stress, lack of exercise, poor sleep, and environmental toxins can exacerbate dietary triggers, compounding the problem.

How Food Affects Inflammation

The relationship between food and inflammation is both simple and profound:

Pro-Inflammatory Foods: Certain foods trigger the production of inflammatory compounds, increasing stress on the body.
Anti-Inflammatory Foods: Rich in antioxidants, vitamins, and healthy fats, these foods neutralize free radicals, support immune function, and reduce inflammatory markers.
Imagine your meals as a balancing act: every bite is an opportunity to either reduce or amplify inflammation.

Basic Principles of Anti-Inflammatory Eating

Focus on Whole Foods
Choose fresh, natural ingredients that are free of additives and preservatives.
Prioritize Nutrient Density
Incorporate foods rich in vitamins, minerals, and antioxidants, like leafy greens and berries.
Balance Healthy Fats
Favor omega-3 fatty acids from fish, nuts, and seeds over omega-6-heavy processed oils.
Limit Sugar and Refined Carbs
Swap sugary snacks and white bread for fruit, whole grains, and other low-glycemic options.

Key Ingredients

Stock your kitchen with these anti-inflammatory superstars:

Turmeric and Ginger: Powerful spices with proven anti-inflammatory properties.
Berries: Rich in antioxidants, which fight oxidative stress and inflammation.
Leafy Greens: Kale, spinach, and other greens are packed with nutrients that reduce inflammation.
Healthy Fats: Olive oil, avocado, and fatty fish provide omega-3s that combat inflammation.
Nuts and Seeds: Almonds, walnuts, flaxseeds, and chia seeds are nutrient-dense and anti-inflammatory.

Foods to Embrace

Build your meals around these inflammation-fighting ingredients:
Fruits and Vegetables: Blueberries, oranges, broccoli, and sweet potatoes.
Whole Grains: Quinoa, brown rice, and oats.
Proteins: Wild-caught salmon, lean poultry, tofu, and beans.
Herbs and Spices: Garlic, cinnamon, and fresh herbs like parsley and basil.

Foods to Limit

Reduce or eliminate these inflammation-promoting foods:
Refined Sugars: Candy, sugary beverages, and desserts.
Processed Foods: Packaged snacks, instant meals, and fast food.
Unhealthy Fats: Trans fats and heavily processed vegetable oils.
Excess Alcohol: Limit to moderate levels, as it can increase inflammation.

Quick Results You Can Expect

One of the most rewarding aspects of adopting an anti-inflammatory diet is how quickly you'll notice improvements. Many people experience:

Increased Energy: Within days, you may feel more alert and less fatigued.
Reduced Bloating: Cutting out inflammatory foods can improve digestion almost immediately.
Better Skin: The antioxidants in anti-inflammatory foods promote a healthy glow.
Less Pain: Over time, inflammation-related joint and muscle pain can decrease significantly.

By sticking to these principles, you'll not only manage inflammation but also pave the way for long-term health and vitality.

BREAKFAST

TURMERIC SPICED SMOOTHIE BOWL

INGREDIENTS

1 cup frozen mango chunks
1 frozen banana
1 cup unsweetened almond milk
1 tsp ground turmeric
1 tsp grated ginger

Start your day with a vibrant and nutritious Turmeric Spiced Smoothie Bowl. Packed with anti-inflammatory ingredients, this bowl is a delicious blend of tropical fruits, plant-based milk, and a touch of turmeric for a morning boost. Topped with your favorite fruits and seeds, it's as satisfying as it is nourishing.

INSTRUCTIONS

1. Combine the frozen mango, banana, almond milk, turmeric, and grated ginger in a powerful blender.
2. Blend on full power until the texture turns smooth and creamy. Adjust the texture consistency by adding more almond milk if needed.
3. Ladle the smoothie into a bowl and add your desired toppings, such as fresh fruit, chia seeds, or shredded coconut.
4. Serve immediately and enjoy your anti-inflammatory morning treat!

Prep Time: 10 mins   **Cook Time:** 00 mins   **Serving:** 2

NUTRITIONAL VALUES (PER SERVING)

Calories: 180, Protein: 2g, Carbohydrates: 38g, Fat: 3g, Fiber: 5g

AVOCADO AND SPAINACH OMELET

INGREDIENTS

- 4 large eggs
- 1 cup fresh spinach leaves
- 1 small avocado, sliced
- 1 tbsp olive oil
- 1 clove garlic, mashed

This Avocado and Spinach Omelet is a protein-packed breakfast perfect for fueling your day. The creamy avocado pairs beautifully with tender spinach, making it a nutritious and satisfying anti-inflammatory meal.

INSTRUCTIONS

1. Heat one tbsp oil in a non-stick skillet over moderate flame. Add mashed garlic and sauté for 1 minute until fragrant.
2. Add spinach and leave until wilted thoroughly for 2 minutes.
3. Grab a shallow bowl, whisk the eggs, and pour them over the spinach. Cook on low heat until the eggs are set, about 4-5 minutes.
4. Slide the omelet onto a plate, fold it, and top with sliced avocado. Serve warm and enjoy!

 Prep Time: 5 mins

 **Cook Time:** 10 mins

 **Serving:** 2

NUTRITIONAL VALUES (PER SERVING)

Calories: 240, Protein: 10g, Carbohydrates: 5g, Fat: 19g, Fiber: 3g

SWEET POTATO AND KALE HASH WITH POACHED EGG

INGREDIENTS

2 medium sweet potatoes, diced
2 cups fresh kale, chopped
2 large eggs
1 tbsp olive oil
1 tsp smoked paprika

This hearty Sweet Potato and Kale Hash with Poached Egg is a nourishing breakfast or brunch option that combines the sweetness of roasted sweet potatoes with earthy kale and a perfectly poached egg.

INSTRUCTIONS

1. Heat one tbsp oil in a skillet over moderate flame.
2. Add diced sweet potatoes and cook until tender and golden, about 10 minutes.
3. Add kale and smoked paprika, and cook until the kale is wilted for about 3 minutes.
4. Meanwhile, poach the eggs in simmering water until the white parts are set and the yolks remain runny for about 3-4 minutes.
5. Serve the sweet potato and kale hash on plates, topped with a poached egg. Enjoy!

Prep Time: 10 mins   **Cook Time:** 15 mins   **Serving:** 2

NUTRITIONAL VALUES (PER SERVING)

Calories: 250, Protein: 8g, Carbohydrates: 25g, Fat: 12g, Fiber: 5g

ANTI-INFLAMMATORY GOLDEN MILK OATS

INGREDIENTS

1 cup rolled oats
2 cups unsweetened almond milk
1 tsp ground turmeric
½ tsp ground cinnamon
1 tsp grated ginger

Warm, creamy, and infused with the soothing flavors of turmeric and spices, these Anti-Inflammatory Golden Milk Oats are the perfect way to kickstart your morning. Packed with antioxidants and fiber, it's a wholesome breakfast to fuel your day.

INSTRUCTIONS

1. In a saucepan, combine almond milk with turmeric, cinnamon, and grated ginger. Heat over moderate flame until warm.
2. Toss in the rolled oats and cook for 5-7 minutes, keep stirring occasionally, until the oats get tender and the mixture is creamy.
3. Divide the oats into bowls and top with your choice of fresh fruit, nuts, or seeds.
4. Serve warm, and enjoy your anti-inflammatory breakfast!

 Prep Time: 5 mins

 **Cook Time:** 10 mins

 Serving: 2

NUTRITIONAL VALUES (PER SERVING)

Calories: 200, Protein: 6g, Carbohydrates: 33g, Fat: 5g, Fiber: 4g

GREEN APPLE AND ALMOND BUTTER TOAST

INGREDIENTS

2 slices whole-grain bread
1 green apple, thinly sliced
2 tbsp almond butter
1 tsp ground cinnamon
1 tsp chia seeds

This quick and satisfying Green Apple and Almond Butter Toast combines crisp apple slices with creamy almond butter on whole-grain toast, making it a deliciously simple anti-inflammatory breakfast or snack.

INSTRUCTIONS

1. Toast the whole-grain bread slices until golden brown.
2. Spread almond butter evenly over each slice.
3. Top with green apple slices and sprinkle with ground cinnamon and chia seeds.
4. Serve immediately and enjoy!

Prep Time:
5 mins

Cook Time:
00 mins

Serving:
2

NUTRITIONAL VALUES (PER SERVING)

Calories: 220, Protein: 6g, Carbohydrates: 28g, Fat: 9g, Fiber: 5g

QUINOA BREAKFAST BOWL WITH ALMONDS

INGREDIENTS

- 1 cup cooked quinoa
- 1 cup unsweetened almond milk
- 1 tsp ground cinnamon
- 2 tbsp slivered almonds
- 1 tsp honey or maple syrup (optional)

This Quinoa Breakfast Bowl with Almonds is a protein-packed, fiber-rich dish that's both hearty and delicious. Topped with slivered almonds, it's a warm and satisfying start to your day.

INSTRUCTIONS

1. In a saucepan, combine the prepared quinoa, almond milk, and cinnamon. Heat over moderate flame until warmed through.
2. Divide the quinoa into bowls and top with slivered almonds and a drizzle of sweetener (honey or maple syrup), if desired. Serve warm and enjoy!

Prep Time:
5 mins

Cook Time:
15 mins

Serving:
2

NUTRITIONAL VALUES (PER SERVING)

Calories: 190, Protein: 6g, Carbohydrates: 27g, Fat: 6g, Fiber: 3g

BANANA AND WALNUT CHIA PUDDING

INGREDIENTS

- 3 tbsp chia seeds
- 1 cup unsweetened almond milk
- 1 ripe banana, mashed
- 2 tbsp chopped walnuts
- ½ tsp ground cinnamon

This creamy and nutrient-dense Banana and Walnut Chia Pudding is packed with omega-3s, fiber, and the natural sweetness of ripe bananas, making it an ideal anti-inflammatory breakfast or snack.

INSTRUCTIONS

1. Grab a shallow bowl and toss the chia seeds, almond milk, mashed banana, and ground cinnamon.
2. Cover and chill for 4 hours (at least) or 6-8 hours until the mixture thickens.
3. Divide into bowls or jars and top with chopped walnuts. Serve and enjoy!

Prep Time: 5 mins   **Cook Time:** 00 mins   **Serving:** 2

NUTRITIONAL VALUES (PER SERVING)

Calories: 210, Protein: 5g, Carbohydrates: 25g, Fat: 10g, Fiber: 7g

COCONUT YOGURT WITH BERRIES AND SEEDS

INGREDIENTS

1 cup unsweetened coconut yogurt
½ cup mixed berries (blueberries, raspberries, strawberries)
1 tbsp chia seeds
1 tbsp flaxseeds
1 tsp honey (optional)

This Coconut Yogurt with Berries and Seeds is a light, refreshing breakfast packed with antioxidants, probiotics, and healthy fats. It's as easy as it is delicious!

INSTRUCTIONS

1. Divide the coconut yogurt between two bowls.
2. Top each with mixed berries, chia seeds, and flaxseeds.
3. Drizzle one tsp honey, if desired, and serve immediately.

Prep Time: 5 mins **Cook Time:** 00 mins **Serving:** 2

NUTRITIONAL VALUES (PER SERVING)

Calories: 180, Protein: 3g, Carbohydrates: 15g, Fat: 10g, Fiber: 5g

LEMON TURMERIC OVERNIGHT OATS

INGREDIENTS

1 cup rolled oats
1 cup unsweetened almond milk
1 tsp ground turmeric
1 tsp lemon zest
1 tsp honey or maple syrup (optional)

Brighten your mornings with Lemon Turmeric Overnight Oats, a creamy and citrusy make-ahead breakfast. Packed with anti-inflammatory properties, it's the perfect blend of health and convenience.

INSTRUCTIONS

1. In a wide-mouth jar or bowl, combine the rolled oats, almond milk, turmeric, lemon zest, and honey (if using).
2. Stir well, cover, and refrigerate overnight.
3. In the morning, stir the oats, divide them between two bowls, and enjoy!

Prep Time: 5 mins   **Cook Time:** 00 mins   **Serving:** 2

NUTRITIONAL VALUES (PER SERVING)

Calories: 180, Protein: 5g, Carbohydrates: 30g, Fat: 4g, Fiber: 5g

SWEET POTATO PANCAKES WITH CINNAMON

INGREDIENTS

- ½ cup mashed sweet potato
- 2 large eggs
- 2 tbsp almond flour
- ½ tsp ground cinnamon
- 1 tsp olive oil (for cooking)

These Sweet Potato Pancakes with Cinnamon are fluffy, nutrient-rich, and lightly spiced, making them a perfect anti-inflammatory breakfast treat for the whole family.

INSTRUCTIONS

1. Grab a shallow bowl and mix the mashed sweet potato, eggs, almond flour, and cinnamon until smooth.
2. Heat one tsp oil in a non-stick skillet over moderate flame.
3. Pour small amounts of batter into the skillet to form pancakes, cooking for 2-3 minutes on one side until golden brown.
4. Serve warm, and enjoy your sweet and savory breakfast!

Prep Time: 10 mins

Cook Time: 10 mins

Serving: 2

NUTRITIONAL VALUES (PER SERVING)
Calories: 180, Protein: 7g, Carbohydrates: 18g, Fat: 8g, Fiber: 3g

APPLE AND ALMOND BUTTER WRAP

INGREDIENTS

- 2 whole-grain wraps
- 1 green apple, thinly sliced
- 2 tbsp almond butter
- 1 tsp ground cinnamon
- 1 tsp chia seeds

This simple and satisfying Apple and Almond Butter Wrap combines crunchy apple slices and creamy almond butter for a quick, healthy breakfast or snack.

INSTRUCTIONS

1. Spread almond butter evenly across each whole-grain wrap.
2. Top with apple slices, sprinkle with ground cinnamon and chia seeds and roll tightly.
3. Slice in half and serve immediately.

 Prep Time: 5 mins

 **Cook Time:** 00 mins

 Serving: 2

NUTRITIONAL VALUES (PER SERVING)

Calories: 220, Protein: 6g, Carbohydrates: 28g, Fat: 9g, Fiber: 4g

TURMERIC AND GINGER INFUSED PORRIDGE

INGREDIENTS

- 1 cup rolled oats
- 2 cups unsweetened almond milk
- 1 tsp ground turmeric
- 1 tsp grated ginger
- 1 tsp honey or maple syrup (optional)

Warm and comforting, this Turmeric and Ginger Infused Porridge combines anti-inflammatory spices with hearty oats for a nourishing start to the day.

INSTRUCTIONS

1. In a saucepan, combine the almond milk, oats, turmeric, and grated ginger.
2. Cook over moderate flame for 5-7 minutes, stirring occasionally, until the oats get a creamy and tender texture.
3. Divide into bowls and drizzle sweetener (honey or maple syrup), if desired. Serve warm and enjoy!

Prep Time: 5 mins   **Cook Time:** 10 mins   **Serving:** 2

NUTRITIONAL VALUES (PER SERVING)

Calories: 190, Protein: 6g, Carbohydrates: 31g, Fat: 4g, Fiber: 5g

AVOCADO AND TOMATO WHOLE GRAIN TOAST

INGREDIENTS

- 2 slices whole-grain bread
- 1 small avocado, mashed
- 1 medium tomato, sliced
- 1 tsp olive oil
- 1 tsp lemon juice

This Avocado and Tomato Whole Grain Toast is a simple and nutritious way to enjoy healthy fats and fresh vegetables in a quick and satisfying breakfast.

INSTRUCTIONS

1. Toast the whole-grain bread slices to your preferred level of crispiness.
2. Spread mashed avocado evenly on each slice, then layer with tomato slices.
3. Drizzle one tsp of oil and lemon juice. Serve immediately and enjoy!

Prep Time: 5 mins **Cook Time:** 00 mins **Serving:** 2

NUTRITIONAL VALUES (PER SERVING)

Calories: 200, Protein: 5g, Carbohydrates: 24g, Fat: 10g, Fiber: 6g

SPICED PEAR AND OAT PARFAIT

INGREDIENTS

1 ripe pear, diced
½ cup rolled oats
1 cup unsweetened coconut yogurt
½ tsp ground cinnamon
1 tsp honey or maple syrup (optional)

This Spiced Pear and Oat Parfait is a delightful combination of warm spiced pears, creamy yogurt, and hearty oats. It's an easy, layered breakfast that's as beautiful as it is

INSTRUCTIONS

1. In a small pan, cook the diced pear with cinnamon over moderate flame for 5 minutes until tender.
2. Cook the rolled oats with 1 cup of water until soft, about 5 minutes. Set aside to cool.
3. In a glass or bowl, layer the oats, coconut yogurt, and spiced pears.
4. Repeat the layers and drizzle sweetener (honey or maple syrup) if desired.
5. Serve chilled, and enjoy your parfait!

Prep Time: 10 mins
Cook Time: 10 mins
Serving: 2

NUTRITIONAL VALUES (PER SERVING)

Calories: 210, Protein: 5g, Carbohydrates: 32g, Fat: 6g, Fiber: 5g

SPINACH AND MUSHROOM EGG MUFFINS

INGREDIENTS

4 large eggs
½ cup fresh spinach, chopped
½ cup mushrooms, diced
1 tbsp olive oil
1 tsp garlic powder

These Spinach and Mushroom Egg Muffins are a protein-packed, make-ahead breakfast perfect for busy mornings. Enjoy them fresh or reheat on the go!

INSTRUCTIONS

1. Preheat oven to 350°F (175°C). Grease a muffin tin with olive oil.
2. Sauté the mushrooms in one tbsp oil for 3 minutes until softened. Add spinach and cook for more 2 minutes.
3. Grab a shallow bowl and whisk the eggs with garlic powder, then mix in the spinach and mushrooms.
4. Divide the muffin mixture into the cups evenly.
5. Bake for 18-20 minutes until the egg muffins are set. Cool slightly, and enjoy!

Prep Time: 10 mins   **Cook Time:** 20 mins   **Serving:** 2

NUTRITIONAL VALUES (PER SERVING)

Calories: 180, Protein: 12g, Carbohydrates: 3g, Fat: 13g, Fiber: 1g

MANGO AND COCONUT CHIA PUDDING

INGREDIENTS

3 tbsp chia seeds
1 cup unsweetened coconut milk
½ cup fresh mango, diced
1 tsp honey (optional)
1 tbsp shredded coconut

This tropical-inspired Mango and Coconut Chia Pudding is creamy, refreshing, and loaded with anti-inflammatory benefits. It's a perfect breakfast or snack option!

INSTRUCTIONS

1. Grab a shallow bowl and toss chia seeds and coconut milk until combined.
2. Cover and chill for 4 hours (at least) or 6-8 hours until thickened.
3. Before serving, stir the chia pudding and divide it into bowls.
4. Top with diced mango and shredded coconut.
5. Drizzle with honey if desired, and enjoy!

Prep Time: 5 mins   **Cook Time:** 00 mins   **Serving:** 2

NUTRITIONAL VALUES (PER SERVING)

Calories: 200, Protein: 4g, Carbohydrates: 16g, Fat: 14g, Fiber: 5g

LEMON AND FLAXSEED PROTEIN PANCAKES

INGREDIENTS

- ½ cup almond flour
- 2 large eggs
- 1 tbsp ground flaxseeds
- 1 tsp lemon zest
- 1 tsp olive oil (for cooking)

These Lemon and Flaxseed Protein Pancakes are light, zesty, and packed with protein and fiber, making them an energizing breakfast choice.

INSTRUCTIONS

1. Grab a shallow bowl and toss almond flour, eggs, ground flaxseeds, and lemon zest until smooth.
2. Heat one tsp oil in a non-stick skillet over moderate flame.
3. Pour small amounts of batter into the skillet to form pancakes.
4. Cook for 2-3 minutes on one side until golden brown.
5. Serve warm and enjoy!

Prep Time: 10 mins   **Cook Time:** 10 mins   **Serving:** 2

NUTRITIONAL VALUES (PER SERVING)

Calories: 210, Protein: 9g, Carbohydrates: 6g, Fat: 17g, Fiber: 3g

MATCHA GREEN TEA SMOOTHIE

INGREDIENTS

1 frozen banana
1 cup unsweetened almond milk
1 tsp matcha powder
½ cup spinach leaves
1 tsp honey (optional)

This creamy and refreshing Matcha Green Tea Smoothie is a blend of antioxidants and natural energy. It's a perfect choice for a quick, health-boosting breakfast.

INSTRUCTIONS

1. Combine the frozen banana, almond milk, matcha powder, and spinach in a powerful blender.
2. Blend on full power until the texture turns smooth and creamy.
3. Taste and add more sweetener honey if desired for extra sweetness.
4. Pour into glasses and serve immediately.
5. Enjoy your vibrant green smoothie!

Prep Time: 5 mins
Cook Time: 00 mins
Serving: 2

NUTRITIONAL VALUES (PER SERVING)

Calories: 140, Protein: 3g, Carbohydrates: 26g, Fat: 2g, Fiber: 3g

GOLDEN MILK BREAKFAST BOWL

INGREDIENTS

1 cup rolled oats
2 cups unsweetened almond milk
1 tsp ground turmeric
½ tsp ground cinnamon
1 tsp honey or maple syrup (optional)

This Golden Milk Breakfast Bowl combines the rich flavors of turmeric and cinnamon with a creamy oatmeal base, creating a warm, anti-inflammatory breakfast that will energize your day.

INSTRUCTIONS

1. Combine the almond milk, turmeric, and cinnamon in a saucepan and heat over moderate flame.
2. Toss in the rolled oats and cook for 5-7 minutes until thick and creamy.
3. Divide the cooked oats into bowls.
4. Drizzle sweetener (honey or maple syrup) if desired.
5. Serve warm and enjoy your golden start to the day!

 Prep Time: 5 mins
 **Cook Time:** 10 mins
 Serving: 2

NUTRITIONAL VALUES (PER SERVING)
Calories: 190, Protein: 6g, Carbohydrates: 31g, Fat: 4g, Fiber: 5g

RASPBERRY AND ALMOND OATMEAL

INGREDIENTS

1 cup rolled oats
2 cups unsweetened almond milk
½ cup fresh raspberries
2 tbsp sliced almonds
1 tsp honey or maple syrup (optional)

This Raspberry and Almond Oatmeal is a delicious and nutritious breakfast packed with antioxidants and healthy fats, perfect for a refreshing start to the day.

INSTRUCTIONS

1. In a saucepan, combine almond milk with oats. Heat over moderate flame and cook until creamy, about 5-7 minutes.
2. Toss in half the raspberries during the last minute of cooking.
3. Divide the oatmeal into bowls and top with remaining raspberries and sliced almonds.
4. Drizzle sweetener (honey or maple syrup) if desired.
5. Serve warm and enjoy your antioxidant-packed breakfast!

Prep Time: 5 mins   **Cook Time:** 10 mins   **Serving:** 2

NUTRITIONAL VALUES (PER SERVING)

Calories: 200, Protein: 6g, Carbohydrates: 30g, Fat: 5g, Fiber: 6g

GINGER AND APPLE SPICED SMOOTHIE

INGREDIENTS

1 green apple, diced
1 frozen banana
1 cup unsweetened almond milk
1 tsp grated ginger
½ tsp ground cinnamon

This refreshing Ginger and Apple Spiced Smoothie is a perfect balance of sweetness and spice. Packed with anti-inflammatory ingredients, it's a quick and energizing breakfast option.

INSTRUCTIONS

1. Combine the green apple, banana, almond milk, grated ginger, and cinnamon in a powerful blender.
2. Blend on full power until the texture turns smooth and creamy.
3. Taste and adjust the sweetness if needed by adding more bananas.
4. Pour into glasses and serve immediately. Enjoy your nutrient-packed smoothie!

Prep Time: 5 mins   **Cook Time:** 00 mins   **Serving:** 2

NUTRITIONAL VALUES (PER SERVING)

Calories: 160, Protein: 2g, Carbohydrates: 35g, Fat: 2g, Fiber: 5g

TURMERIC SCRAMBLED EGGS WITH SPINACH

INGREDIENTS

4 large eggs
1 cup fresh spinach leaves
1 tsp ground turmeric
1 tbsp olive oil
1 clove garlic, mashed

Brighten up your breakfast with these Turmeric Scrambled Eggs with Spinach, a simple, flavorful dish packed with protein and anti-inflammatory benefits.

INSTRUCTIONS

1. Heat one tbsp oil in a skillet over moderate flame and sauté the garlic for 1 minute.
2. Add spinach and leave until wilted thoroughly for 2 minutes.
3. Grab a shallow bowl and whisk the eggs with turmeric until combined.
4. Pour the egg mixture and scramble gently until fully cooked.
5. Serve warm and enjoy your vibrant, healthy breakfast!

Prep Time: 5 mins
Cook Time: 5 mins
Serving: 2

NUTRITIONAL VALUES (PER SERVING)

Calories: 190, Protein: 12g, Carbohydrates: 3g, Fat: 15g, Fiber: 1g

ROASTED SWEET POTATO AND AVOCADO MASH

INGREDIENTS

1 medium sweet potato
1 small avocado, mashed
1 tbsp olive oil
1 tsp ground cumin
1 tsp lemon juice

This Roasted Sweet Potato and Avocado Mash is a simple, nutrient-packed breakfast that combines the sweetness of roasted sweet potato with creamy avocado for a satisfying and anti-inflammatory meal.

INSTRUCTIONS

1. Preheat oven to 400°F (200°C). Arrange the baking sheet with parchment paper.
2. Slice the sweet potato into rounds, drizzle one tbsp oil, and sprinkle with cumin. Roast for 20-25 minutes until tender.
3. While the sweet potato roasts, mash the avocado with lemon juice in a small bowl.
4. Arrange the roasted sweet potato slices on a plate and top each with a dollop of avocado mash.
5. Serve warm, and enjoy your flavorful breakfast!

Prep Time: 10 mins
Cook Time: 25 mins
Serving: 2

NUTRITIONAL VALUES (PER SERVING)

Calories: 200, Protein: 3g, Carbohydrates: 25g, Fat: 10g, Fiber: 6g

GREEK-INSPIRED EGG WRAPS

INGREDIENTS

- 4 large eggs
- 1 cup fresh spinach, chopped
- ½ cup cherry tomatoes, halved
- 2 tbsp crumbled feta cheese
- 1 tbsp olive oil

These Greek-Inspired Egg Wraps are a delicious and protein-rich breakfast featuring classic Mediterranean flavors like spinach, tomatoes, and feta wrapped in fluffy eggs.

INSTRUCTIONS

1. Whisk the eggs in a deep-bottom bowl until smooth.
2. Heat one tbsp oil in a non-stick skillet over moderate flame and ladle in half of the eggs to form a thin layer.
3. Once the eggs are set, add spinach, tomatoes, and feta to one side of the egg wrap. Fold over and cook for 1 minute.
4. Repeat with the remaining eggs and ingredients to make a second wrap.
5. Serve warm and enjoy the fresh Mediterranean flavors!

Prep Time: 5 mins **Cook Time:** 10 mins **Serving:** 2

NUTRITIONAL VALUES (PER SERVING)

Calories: 220, Protein: 14g, Carbohydrates: 4g, Fat: 16g, Fiber: 1g

CINNAMON AND PUMPKIN BREAKFAST PORRIDGE

INGREDIENTS

1 cup rolled oats
2 cups unsweetened almond milk
½ cup pumpkin puree
1 tsp ground cinnamon
1 tsp honey or maple syrup (optional)

This cozy Cinnamon and Pumpkin Breakfast Porridge is a hearty and flavorful dish, perfect for fall mornings or any time you crave warm and comforting flavors.

INSTRUCTIONS

1. In a saucepan, combine almond milk, oats, pumpkin puree, and cinnamon. Heat over moderate flame.
2. Stir occasionally and cook for 5-7 minutes until thick and creamy.
3. Divide the porridge into bowls.
4. Drizzle sweetener (honey or maple syrup) if desired for added sweetness.
5. Serve warm and enjoy your fall-inspired breakfast!

Prep Time: 5 mins
Cook Time: 10 mins
Serving: 2

NUTRITIONAL VALUES (PER SERVING)

Calories: 190, Protein: 6g, Carbohydrates: 32g, Fat: 4g, Fiber: 5g

LUNCH

GRILLED SALMON WITH QUINOA AND SPINACH

INGREDIENTS

- 2 salmon fillets (4-6 oz each)
- 1 cup cooked quinoa
- 2 cups fresh spinach
- 1 tbsp olive oil
- 1 tsp lemon juice

This Grilled Salmon with Quinoa and Spinach is a light yet satisfying meal, loaded with protein and omega-3s. Paired with fluffy quinoa and nutrient-dense spinach, it's a perfectly balanced lunch option.

INSTRUCTIONS

1. Heat a grill pan over moderate flame and brush with olive oil.
2. Season the salmon with salt and crushed pepper, then grill for 4-5 minutes on one side until cooked through.
3. In a skillet, sauté spinach with a drizzle of olive oil until wilted.
4. Divide cooked quinoa and sautéed spinach between two plates, then top each with grilled salmon.
5. Drizzle one tsp juice and serve warm.

Prep Time: 10 mins
Cook Time: 15 mins
Serving: 2

NUTRITIONAL VALUES (PER SERVING)

Calories: 350, Protein: 32g, Carbohydrates: 20g, Fat: 15g, Fiber: 3g

ROASTED VEGETABLE AND CHICKPEA BOWL

INGREDIENTS

1 cup chickpeas (cooked or canned, rinsed and drained)
1 medium zucchini, diced
1 red bell pepper, diced
1 cup cherry tomatoes
1 tbsp olive oil

Packed with vibrant flavors, this Roasted Vegetable and Chickpea Bowl is a hearty and wholesome lunch that's rich in plant-based protein and fiber.

INSTRUCTIONS

1. Preheat oven to 400°F (200°C). Arrange the baking sheet with parchment paper.
2. Toss chickpeas, zucchini, bell pepper, and cherry tomatoes with olive oil. Spread evenly on the parchment paper-arranged baking sheet.
3. Roast for 23-25 minutes until vegetables get tender and slightly charred.
4. Divide roasted veggies and chickpeas into bowls.
5. Serve warm, and enjoy your nutrient-packed meal!

Prep Time: 10 mins
Cook Time: 25 mins
Serving: 2

NUTRITIONAL VALUES (PER SERVING)

Calories: 280, Protein: 10g, Carbohydrates: 35g, Fat: 10g, Fiber: 8g

TURKEY AND AVOCADO LETTUCE WRAPS

INGREDIENTS

6 large lettuce leaves
4 oz cooked turkey breast, sliced
1 small avocado, sliced
1 medium tomato, diced
1 tsp Dijon mustard

These Turkey and Avocado Lettuce Wraps are a quick and delicious low-carb lunch option, combining lean protein with creamy avocado and crisp lettuce.

INSTRUCTIONS

1. Lay the lettuce leaves flat and spread a small amount of Dijon mustard on each.
2. Layer with turkey slices, avocado, and diced tomato.
3. Roll each lettuce leaf tightly to form wraps.
4. Secure with toothpicks if necessary.
5. Serve immediately and enjoy!

Prep Time: 10 mins
Cook Time: 00 mins
Serving: 2

NUTRITIONAL VALUES (PER SERVING)

Calories: 220, Protein: 20g, Carbohydrates: 8g, Fat: 13g, Fiber: 4g

CHICKEN SALAD WITH OLIVE OIL DRESSING

INGREDIENTS

2 cups cooked chicken breast, shredded
2 cups mixed greens
1 cucumber, sliced
1 tbsp olive oil
1 tsp lemon juice

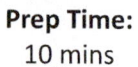

This Chicken Salad with Olive Oil Dressing is a fresh, protein-packed meal featuring juicy chicken, crunchy vegetables, and a light dressing for a perfectly balanced lunch.

INSTRUCTIONS

1. Grab a shallow bowl and combine shredded chicken, mixed greens, and cucumber slices.
2. Toss olive oil and lemon juice to make the dressing.
3. Pour lemon oil dressing over the salad and toss well to coat.
4. Divide the salad between two shallow plates or bowls.
5. Serve immediately and enjoy your fresh, healthy meal!

Prep Time: 10 mins
Cook Time: 10 mins
Serving: 2

NUTRITIONAL VALUES (PER SERVING)

Calories: 250, Protein: 30g, Carbohydrates: 5g, Fat: 10g, Fiber: 2g

SPICY QUINOA SALAD WITH KALE AND NUTS

INGREDIENTS

1 cup cooked quinoa
2 cups kale, chopped
2 tbsp mixed nuts (e.g., almonds, walnuts)
1 tbsp olive oil
½ tsp chili flakes

This Spicy Quinoa Salad with Kale and Nuts is a flavorful and crunchy dish that's loaded with protein, fiber, and a subtle kick of spice for an energizing lunch.

INSTRUCTIONS

1. Heat one tbsp oil in a skillet and sauté kale for 3-4 minutes until tender.
2. Grab a shallow bowl and combine cooked quinoa, sautéed kale, and mixed nuts.
3. Sprinkle chili flakes over the salad for a spicy kick.
4. Toss everything together and divide into bowls.
5. Serve warm or chilled, and enjoy!

Prep Time: 10 mins
Cook Time: 10 mins
Serving: 2

NUTRITIONAL VALUES (PER SERVING)

Calories: 280, Protein: 8g, Carbohydrates: 30g, Fat: 12g, Fiber: 5g

GRILLED CHICKEN WITH ZUCCHINI NOODLES

INGREDIENTS

2 medium zucchinis, spiralized
2 chicken breasts
1 tbsp olive oil
1 tsp garlic powder
1 tsp lemon juice

This Grilled Chicken with Zucchini Noodles is a low-carb, high-protein lunch option packed with fresh flavors and nutritious ingredients. The zucchini noodles provide a light and refreshing twist to this classic dish.

INSTRUCTIONS

1. Heat a grill pan over moderate flame and brush with olive oil.
2. Season the breast meat with garlic powder and grill for 6-7 minutes on one side or until fully cooked.
3. In a skillet, sauté the zucchini noodles with one tbsp oil for 2-3 minutes until slightly tender.
4. Slice the grilled breast meat and serve over the zucchini noodles.
5. Drizzle one tsp lemon juice and enjoy your flavorful, healthy meal!

Prep Time: 10 mins
Cook Time: 15 mins
Serving: 2

NUTRITIONAL VALUES (PER SERVING)

Calories: 280, Protein: 34g, Carbohydrates: 6g, Fat: 12g, Fiber: 2g

AVOCADO AND CUCUMBER SUSHI ROLLS

INGREDIENTS

4 large nori sheets
1 avocado, sliced
1 cucumber, julienned
1 cup shredded carrots
1 tbsp sesame seeds

These Avocado and Cucumber Sushi Rolls are a light and refreshing lunch option, offering all the flavors of sushi in a quick and easy-to-make format without the need for fish or rice.

INSTRUCTIONS

1. Lay a nori sheet on a flat surface and spread a thin layer of avocado slices evenly across the bottom edge.
2. Add cucumber and shredded carrots on top of the avocado.
3. Roll the nori sheet tightly from the bottom, using your fingers to press and seal the edge.
4. Slice the rolls into bite-sized pieces and sprinkle with sesame seeds.
5. Serve immediately and enjoy your plant-based sushi!

Prep Time: 15 mins
Cook Time: 00 mins
Serving: 2

NUTRITIONAL VALUES (PER SERVING)

Calories: 190, Protein: 4g, Carbohydrates: 14g, Fat: 14g, Fiber: 5g

SWEET POTATO AND LENTIL CURRY

INGREDIENTS

1 medium sweet potato, diced
½ cup dried lentils
1 cup coconut milk
1 tsp ground turmeric
1 tsp curry powder

This hearty Sweet Potato and Lentil Curry is a comforting, protein-packed dish loaded with warm spices and anti-inflammatory ingredients. It's a delicious and filling lunch.

INSTRUCTIONS

1. In a deep-bottom pot, add diced sweet potato, lentils, and coconut milk. Get it to a boil.
2. Decrease the stove heat and simmer for 20-25 minutes, stirring occasionally, until the sweet potato is tender and the lentils are cooked.
3. Toss in turmeric and curry powder, mixing well to combine.
4. Adjust consistency by adding a little water if needed.
5. Serve warm, and enjoy your flavorful curry!

Prep Time: 10 mins
Cook Time: 25 mins
Serving: 2

NUTRITIONAL VALUES (PER SERVING)

Calories: 300, Protein: 12g, Carbohydrates: 40g, Fat: 10g, Fiber: 8g

SALMON AND CUCUMBER SALAD

INGREDIENTS

- 2 cups mixed greens
- 1 cup cucumber slices
- 4 oz cooked salmon, flaked
- 1 tbsp olive oil
- 1 tsp lemon juice

This Salmon and Cucumber Salad is a refreshing and protein-rich dish that combines tender salmon with crisp cucumber, making it a perfect light lunch option.

INSTRUCTIONS

1. In a large, deep-bottom bowl, combine mixed greens and cucumber slices.
2. Add flaked salmon on top of the salad.
3. Drizzle with one tbsp oil and lemon juice.
4. Toss gently to combine and coat the ingredients.
5. Serve immediately and enjoy your fresh, nutritious salad!

Prep Time: 10 mins
Cook Time: 00 mins
Serving: 2

NUTRITIONAL VALUES (PER SERVING)

Calories: 250, Protein: 22g, Carbohydrates: 6g, Fat: 16g, Fiber: 2g

TURMERIC CHICKPEA BUDDHA BOWL

INGREDIENTS

1 cup cooked chickpeas
1 cup roasted sweet potato chunks
2 cups mixed greens
1 tbsp olive oil
1 tsp ground turmeric

This Turmeric Chickpea Buddha Bowl is a nourishing, plant-based meal filled with vibrant colors and flavors. The roasted chickpeas add a satisfying crunch to this wholesome dish.

INSTRUCTIONS

1. Preheat oven to 400°F (200°C). Toss chickpeas and sweet potato chunks with olive oil and turmeric.
2. Spread the mixture on the parchment paper-arranged baking sheet and roast for 20 minutes, stirring halfway through.
3. Arrange mixed greens in two bowls.
4. Top with roasted chickpeas and sweet potato.
5. Serve warm or chilled, and enjoy your flavorful Buddha bowl!

Prep Time: 10 mins
Cook Time: 20 mins
Serving: 2

NUTRITIONAL VALUES (PER SERVING)

Calories: 280, Protein: 8g, Carbohydrates: 35g, Fat: 10g, Fiber: 7g

BAKED FALAFEL WITH TAHINI DRIZZLE

INGREDIENTS

1 cup cooked chickpeas
¼ cup chopped parsley
1 clove garlic, mashed
1 tbsp olive oil
1 tsp ground cumin

These Baked Falafel with Tahini Drizzle are crispy, flavorful, and packed with plant-based protein. Baking instead of frying makes them a healthy and satisfying lunch option.

INSTRUCTIONS

1. Preheat oven to 375°F (190°C). Arrange the baking sheet with parchment paper.
2. In a food processor, blend chickpeas, parsley, garlic, olive oil, and cumin until a coarse dough forms.
3. Form the mixture into small patties and place them on the parchment paper-arranged baking sheet.
4. Bake for 18-20 minutes, flip after halftime has passed, until golden and firm.
5. Serve with a drizzle of tahini, and enjoy!

Prep Time: 10 mins
Cook Time: 20 mins
Serving: 2

NUTRITIONAL VALUES (PER SERVING)

Calories: 250, Protein: 8g, Carbohydrates: 30g, Fat: 10g, Fiber: 7g

WARM BEET AND SPINACH SALAD

INGREDIENTS

2 medium beets, peeled and diced
2 cups fresh spinach
1 tbsp olive oil
1 tsp balsamic vinegar
1 tsp Dijon mustard

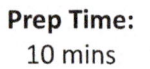

This Warm Beet and Spinach Salad is a vibrant and nutritious dish, combining earthy beets with fresh spinach for a perfect balance of flavors and textures.

INSTRUCTIONS

1. Preheat oven to 400°F (200°C). Toss diced beets with olive oil and roast for 20 minutes until tender.
2. Take a small shallow bowl and toss balsamic vinegar and Dijon mustard for the dressing.
3. Place spinach in a large deep-bottom bowl and add warm roasted beets.
4. Drizzle balsamic vinegar dressing over the salad and toss gently to combine.
5. Serve immediately and enjoy your nutritious warm salad!

Prep Time: 10 mins
Cook Time: 20 mins
Serving: 2

NUTRITIONAL VALUES (PER SERVING)

Calories: 190, Protein: 4g, Carbohydrates: 18g, Fat: 10g, Fiber: 5g

TOMATO AND AVOCADO GAZPACHO

INGREDIENTS

2 medium tomatoes, chopped
1 small avocado
1 clove garlic
1 tbsp olive oil
1 tsp lemon juice

This Tomato and Avocado Gazpacho is a refreshing and creamy cold soup, perfect for hot days. It's loaded with anti-inflammatory ingredients and vibrant flavors.

INSTRUCTIONS

1. In a blender, combine tomatoes, avocado, garlic, olive oil, and lemon juice.
2. Blend on full power until the texture turns smooth and creamy.
3. Taste and adjust seasoning with salt and crushed pepper if needed.
4. Chill in the refrigerator for 15 minutes or serve immediately.
5. Spread fresh herbs if desired, and enjoy!

Prep Time: 10 mins
Cook Time: 00 mins
Serving: 2

NUTRITIONAL VALUES (PER SERVING)

Calories: 180, Protein: 3g, Carbohydrates: 12g, Fat: 15g, Fiber: 6g

LEMON HERB SHRIMP SALAD

INGREDIENTS

1 cup cooked shrimp
2 cups mixed greens
1 tbsp olive oil
1 tsp lemon juice
1 tsp chopped fresh parsley

This light and flavorful Lemon Herb Shrimp Salad combines tender shrimp with crisp greens and a tangy herb dressing for a refreshing lunch.

INSTRUCTIONS

1. In a skillet, heat one tbsp oil over moderate flame and sauté the shrimp for 2-3 minutes until heated through.
2. In a large, deep-bottom bowl, combine mixed greens and parsley.
3. Add shrimp and drizzle one tsp lemon juice. Toss gently to coat with the dressing.
4. Serve immediately and enjoy your fresh, herb-infused salad!

Prep Time: 10 mins
Cook Time: 5 mins
Serving: 2

NUTRITIONAL VALUES (PER SERVING)

Calories: 200, Protein: 18g, Carbohydrates: 5g, Fat: 12g, Fiber: 2g

CAULIFLOWER RICE STIR-FRY WITH TOFU

INGREDIENTS

- 1 cup cauliflower rice
- ½ cup diced tofu
- 1 cup mixed vegetables (e.g., bell peppers, carrots, peas)
- 1 tbsp olive oil
- 1 tsp soy sauce

This Cauliflower Rice Stir-Fry with Tofu is a quick and nutrient-packed meal, combining protein-rich tofu with vibrant vegetables and low-carb cauliflower rice.

INSTRUCTIONS

1. Heat one tbsp oil in a skillet over moderate flame and sauté tofu until golden, about 5 minutes.
2. Add mixed veggies and cook for 3-4 minutes until tender.
3. Toss in the cauliflower rice and soy sauce, cooking for an additional 2-3 minutes.
4. Toss everything together to combine evenly.
5. Serve warm, and enjoy your quick and healthy stir-fry!

Prep Time: 10 mins
Cook Time: 10 mins
Serving: 2

NUTRITIONAL VALUES (PER SERVING)

Calories: 180, Protein: 10g, Carbohydrates: 12g, Fat: 10g, Fiber: 4g

COCONUT CURRY LENTIL SOUP

INGREDIENTS

- ½ cup dried lentils
- 1 cup coconut milk
- 1 cup vegetable broth
- 1 tsp curry powder
- 1 tsp grated ginger

This creamy and flavorful Coconut Curry Lentil Soup is packed with protein and fiber, making it a comforting, anti-inflammatory lunch option perfect for any day.

INSTRUCTIONS

1. In a deep-bottom pot, combine lentils, coconut milk, and vegetable broth. Get it to a boil.
2. Decrease the stove heat to a simmer and toss in curry powder and grated ginger.
3. Cook for 20-25 minutes, keep stirring occasionally, until lentils are tender.
4. Adjust the seasoning with salt and crushed pepper if needed.
5. Serve warm, and enjoy this comforting soup!

Prep Time: 10 mins
Cook Time: 25 mins
Serving: 2

NUTRITIONAL VALUES (PER SERVING)

Calories: 280, Protein: 10g, Carbohydrates: 28g, Fat: 12g, Fiber: 7g

ROASTED SQUASH AND QUINOA SALAD

INGREDIENTS

1 cup butternut squash, diced
1 cup cooked quinoa
2 cups mixed greens
1 tbsp olive oil
1 tsp balsamic vinegar

This Roasted Squash and Quinoa Salad is a vibrant and hearty dish that combines roasted butternut squash with protein-rich quinoa, perfect for a light yet satisfying meal.

INSTRUCTIONS

1. Preheat oven to 400°F (200°C). Toss diced butternut squash with one tbsp oil and roast for 20-25 minutes until tender.
2. In a large, deep-bottom bowl, combine cooked quinoa, mixed greens, and roasted squash.
3. Drizzle one tsp balsamic vinegar and toss to combine.
4. Divide into two servings and spread optional nuts or seeds if desired.
5. Serve warm and enjoy!

Prep Time: 10 mins
Cook Time: 25 mins
Serving: 2

NUTRITIONAL VALUES (PER SERVING)

Calories: 250, Protein: 7g, Carbohydrates: 35g, Fat: 8g, Fiber: 6g

GRILLED EGGPLANT AND CHICKPEA WRAPS

INGREDIENTS

1 medium eggplant, sliced
1 cup cooked chickpeas
2 whole-grain wraps
1 tbsp olive oil
1 tsp ground cumin

These Grilled Eggplant and Chickpea Wraps are bursting with Mediterranean flavors. They're a delicious plant-based option perfect for a quick lunch.

INSTRUCTIONS

1. Heat a grill pan over moderate flame and brush eggplant slices with olive oil. Grill for 3-4 minutes on one side until tender.
2. Grab a shallow bowl and toss chickpeas with cumin.
3. Place grilled eggplant slices and chickpeas onto the center of each wrap.
4. Roll the wraps tightly, then slice in half if desired.
5. Serve immediately and enjoy your flavorful Mediterranean lunch!

Prep Time: 10 mins
Cook Time: 15 mins
Serving: 2

NUTRITIONAL VALUES (PER SERVING)

Calories: 300, Protein: 10g, Carbohydrates: 40g, Fat: 12g, Fiber: 8g

GINGER LIME SHRIMP BOWLS

INGREDIENTS

1 cup cooked shrimp
1 cup cooked quinoa
1 cup cucumber slices
1 tbsp lime juice
1 tsp grated ginger

These zesty Ginger Lime Shrimp Bowls are packed with fresh flavors and make a light, protein-rich lunch that's perfect for warm days.

INSTRUCTIONS

1. Grab a shallow bowl and combine cooked shrimp with lime juice and grated ginger. Toss to coat.
2. Divide the cooked quinoa and cucumber slices between two bowls.
3. Top each bowl with the seasoned shrimp.
4. Drizzle with additional lime juice if desired.
5. Serve immediately and enjoy your fresh, flavorful bowl!

Prep Time: 10 mins
Cook Time: 5 mins
Serving: 2

NUTRITIONAL VALUES (PER SERVING)

Calories: 250, Protein: 20g, Carbohydrates: 22g, Fat: 6g, Fiber: 2g

GRILLED TURKEY PATTIES WITH CUCUMBER SALAD

INGREDIENTS

8 oz ground turkey
1 tsp garlic powder
1 tbsp olive oil
1 cup cucumber slices
1 tsp lemon juice

These Grilled Turkey Patties with Cucumber Salad are a light and flavorful option for a high-protein, anti-inflammatory lunch.

INSTRUCTIONS

1. Mix ground turkey with garlic powder and form into small patties.
2. Heat one tbsp oil in a grill pan over moderate flame and grill the patties for 4-5 minutes on one side until fully cooked.
3. Grab a shallow bowl and toss cucumber slices with lemon juice.
4. Serve the grilled turkey patties alongside the cucumber salad.
5. Enjoy your simple and nutritious meal!

Prep Time: 10 mins
Cook Time: 10 mins
Serving: 2

NUTRITIONAL VALUES (PER SERVING)

Calories: 250, Protein: 28g, Carbohydrates: 3g, Fat: 14g, Fiber: 1g

STEAMED VEGGIE WITH SESAME DRESSING

INGREDIENTS

2 cups mixed vegetables (e.g., broccoli, carrots, and snap peas)
1 tbsp sesame oil
1 tsp soy sauce
1 tsp rice vinegar
1 tsp sesame seeds

This Steamed Veggie with Sesame Dressing is a simple, nutritious dish that pairs crisp, steamed vegetables with a rich sesame dressing for a delicious and healthy lunch option.

INSTRUCTIONS

1. Steam the mixed vegetables for 5 minutes until tender but still crisp.
2. Take a small shallow bowl and toss sesame oil, soy sauce, and rice vinegar for the dressing.
3. Transfer the steamed vegetables to a plate. Drizzle the sesame dressing over the veggies and sprinkle with sesame seeds.
4. Serve warm, and enjoy this light and flavorful dish!

Prep Time: 10 mins
Cook Time: 5 mins
Serving: 2

NUTRITIONAL VALUES (PER SERVING)

Calories: 120, Protein: 3g, Carbohydrates: 12g, Fat: 7g, Fiber: 4g

SPICY LENTIL AND TOMATO SOUP

INGREDIENTS

- ½ cup dried lentils
- 1 cup canned diced tomatoes
- 2 cups vegetable broth
- 1 tsp ground cumin
- ½ tsp chili flakes

This hearty Spicy Lentil and Tomato Soup is a comforting and filling dish packed with protein, fiber, and anti-inflammatory spices for a warming lunch.

INSTRUCTIONS

1. In a deep-bottom pot, combine lentils, diced tomatoes, and vegetable broth. Get it to a boil.
2. Toss in ground cumin and chili flakes. Decrease the stove heat to a simmer.
3. Cook for 20 minutes, stirring occasionally, until lentils are tender.
4. Adjust seasoning with salt and crushed pepper if needed. Serve warm, and enjoy this spicy, hearty soup!

Prep Time: 10 mins
Cook Time: 20 mins
Serving: 2

NUTRITIONAL VALUES (PER SERVING)

Calories: 200, Protein: 10g, Carbohydrates: 30g, Fat: 2g, Fiber: 9g

ZUCCHINI AND SWEET POTATO FRITTERS

INGREDIENTS

- 1 cup grated zucchini
- 1 cup grated sweet potato
- 1 large egg
- 2 tbsp almond flour
- 1 tbsp olive oil

These Zucchini and Sweet Potato Fritters are crispy, flavorful, and packed with nutrients. Perfect for a light lunch or a side dish, they're easy to prepare and loaded with anti-inflammatory ingredients.

INSTRUCTIONS

1. Grab a shallow bowl and mix grated zucchini, sweet potato, egg, and almond flour until well combined.
2. Heat one tbsp oil in a skillet over moderate flame.
3. Scoop the mixture into the skillet, forming small patties. Flatten slightly with a spatula.
4. Cook for 3-4 minutes on one side until golden brown and crispy.
5. Serve warm, and enjoy your flavorful fritters!

Prep Time: 10 mins
Cook Time: 10 mins
Serving: 2

NUTRITIONAL VALUES (PER SERVING)

Calories: 180, Protein: 6g, Carbohydrates: 18g, Fat: 10g, Fiber: 4g

GINGER CHICKEN AND BROWN RICE BOWL

INGREDIENTS

1 cup cooked brown rice
6 oz chicken breast, diced
1 tsp grated ginger
1 tbsp olive oil
1 cup steamed broccoli

This Ginger Chicken and Brown Rice Bowl is a satisfying, protein-packed dish that combines tender chicken with aromatic ginger and hearty brown rice for a balanced

INSTRUCTIONS

1. Heat one tbsp oil in a skillet over moderate flame and cook the chicken until browned about 8-10 minutes.
2. Add grated ginger and sauté for 1-2 minutes until fragrant.
3. Steam broccoli until tender but crisp, about 5 minutes.
4. Divide the prepared brown rice into two bowls and top it with chicken and broccoli.
5. Serve warm, and enjoy your flavorful, protein-rich meal!

Prep Time: 10 mins
Cook Time: 20 mins
Serving: 2

NUTRITIONAL VALUES (PER SERVING)

Calories: 320, Protein: 28g, Carbohydrates: 30g, Fat: 8g, Fiber: 4g

ROASTED VEGGIE WRAPS WITH HUMMUS

INGREDIENTS

1 cup mixed vegetables (e.g., zucchini, bell peppers, and onions), sliced
2 whole-grain wraps
2 tbsp hummus
1 tbsp olive oil
1 tsp paprika

These Roasted Veggie Wraps with Hummus are packed with flavor and nutrients, featuring roasted vegetables and creamy hummus wrapped in whole-grain tortillas for a delicious lunch option.

INSTRUCTIONS

1. Preheat oven to 400°F (200°C). Toss sliced vegetables with olive oil and paprika.
2. Spread the veggies on the parchment paper-arranged baking sheet and roast for 20 minutes.
3. Spread hummus evenly over each wrap. Add roasted veggies and roll the wraps tightly.
4. Slice in half and serve warm or at room temperature. Enjoy!

Prep Time: 10 mins
Cook Time: 20 mins
Serving: 2

NUTRITIONAL VALUES (PER SERVING)

Calories: 240, Protein: 6g, Carbohydrates: 28g, Fat: 10g, Fiber: 5g

DINNER

BAKED COD WITH TOMATO AND BASIL SAUCE

INGREDIENTS

2 cod fillets (4-6 oz each)
1 cup canned diced tomatoes
1 tbsp olive oil
1 clove garlic, mashed
2 tbsp fresh basil, chopped

This Baked Cod with Tomato and Basil Sauce is a light and flavorful dinner option. Tender cod fillets are baked in a simple tomato sauce infused with fresh basil for a quick and healthy meal.

INSTRUCTIONS

1. Preheat oven to 375°F (190°C).
2. In a baking dish, combine diced tomatoes, mashed garlic, and olive oil. Stir to mix.
3. Place the cod fillets on top of the tomato mixture and sprinkle with salt and crushed pepper.
4. Bake for 20 minutes until the cod is done thoroughly and flakes easily.
5. Spread fresh basil and serve warm. Enjoy!

Prep Time: 10 mins
Cook Time: 20 mins
Serving: 2

NUTRITIONAL VALUES (PER SERVING)

Calories: 200, Protein: 25g, Carbohydrates: 8g, Fat: 7g, Fiber: 2g

GINGER SESAME SHRIMP STIR-FRY WITH ZUCCHINI

INGREDIENTS

1 cup shrimp, peeled and deveined
1 medium zucchini, sliced into thin rounds
1 tbsp sesame oil
1 tsp grated ginger
1 tsp soy sauce

This Ginger Sesame Shrimp Stir-Fry with Zucchini is a quick and flavorful dinner that combines juicy shrimp, crisp zucchini, and a hint of ginger for a delicious, anti-inflammatory meal.

INSTRUCTIONS

1. Heat one tbsp sesame oil in a skillet over moderate flame and sauté the grated ginger for 1 minute.
2. Add shrimp and sear for 2-3 minutes on one side until pink and fully cooked.
3. Add zucchini slices and stir-fry for 3-4 minutes until tender-crisp.
4. Drizzle soy sauce over the shrimp and zucchini, tossing to coat.
5. Serve warm, and enjoy your quick and healthy stir-fry!

Prep Time: 10 mins
Cook Time: 10 mins
Serving: 2

NUTRITIONAL VALUES (PER SERVING)

Calories: 180, Protein: 20g, Carbohydrates: 5g, Fat: 9g, Fiber: 2g

TURMERIC-SPICED ROASTED CAULIFLOWER AND TOFU

INGREDIENTS

1 cup cauliflower florets
½ cup tofu, cubed
1 tbsp olive oil
1 tsp ground turmeric
½ tsp paprika

This Turmeric-Spiced Roasted Cauliflower and Tofu is a vibrant and protein-rich dish that's as delicious as it is nourishing. The combination of roasted cauliflower and crispy tofu makes for a hearty dinner.

INSTRUCTIONS

1. Preheat oven to 400°F (200°C). Arrange the baking sheet with parchment paper.
2. Toss the cauliflower florets and tofu cubes with one tbsp oil, turmeric, and paprika in a bowl.
3. Spread the mixture evenly on the parchment paper-arranged baking sheet and roast for 20-25 minutes; flip after halftime has passed.
4. Remove from the oven once golden and tender. Serve warm and enjoy your flavorful, protein-packed dinner!

Prep Time: 10 mins
Cook Time: 25 mins
Serving: 2

NUTRITIONAL VALUES (PER SERVING)

Calories: 220, Protein: 10g, Carbohydrates: 12g, Fat: 14g, Fiber: 4g

SALMON WITH DILL AND LEMON SAUCE

INGREDIENTS

2 salmon fillets (4-6 oz each)
1 tbsp olive oil
1 tbsp fresh dill, chopped
1 tsp lemon juice
1 clove garlic, mashed

This Salmon with Dill and Lemon Sauce is a classic and elegant dinner dish. The tangy lemon and fresh dill elevate the rich flavor of the salmon, making it a simple yet impressive meal.

INSTRUCTIONS

1. Heat one tbsp oil in a skillet over moderate flame. Add salmon fillets skin-side down and cook for 4-5 minutes.
2. Flip the fillets and cook for more 4-5 minutes until the salmon is done thoroughly.
3. Take a small shallow bowl and mix lemon juice, dill, and mashed garlic.
4. Drizzle the sauce over the cooked salmon.
5. Serve immediately and enjoy your fresh, flavorful dinner!

Prep Time: 5 mins
Cook Time: 15 mins
Serving: 2

NUTRITIONAL VALUES (PER SERVING)

Calories: 300, Protein: 30g, Carbohydrates: 2g, Fat: 20g, Fiber: 0g

CAULIFLOWER AND CHICKPEA STEW

INGREDIENTS

1 cup cauliflower florets
1 cup cooked chickpeas
1 cup vegetable broth
1 cup canned diced tomatoes
1 tsp ground cumin

This Cauliflower and Chickpea Stew is a hearty, plant-based dinner option filled with warming spices and anti-inflammatory ingredients. It's perfect for a cozy and nourishing evening meal.

INSTRUCTIONS

1. Heat a deep-bottom pot over moderate flame and add cauliflower florets, chickpeas, and cumin.
2. Ladle in the vegetable broth and canned diced tomatoes, stirring to combine.
3. Get it to a boil, then decrease the stove heat and simmer for 23-25 minutes until the cauliflower is tender.
4. Adjust seasoning with salt and crushed pepper if needed. Serve warm, and enjoy your comforting, protein-rich stew!

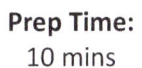

Prep Time: 10 mins
Cook Time: 25 mins
Serving: 2

NUTRITIONAL VALUES (PER SERVING)

Calories: 240, Protein: 10g, Carbohydrates: 30g, Fat: 6g, Fiber: 8g

LENTIL CURRY WITH SWEET POTATOES

INGREDIENTS

½ cup dried lentils
1 cup sweet potato, diced
1 cup coconut milk
1 tsp curry powder
1 tsp ground turmeric

This Lentil Curry with Sweet Potatoes is a hearty, anti-inflammatory dish filled with warm spices and nutrient-rich ingredients. It's a comforting and satisfying dinner option.

INSTRUCTIONS

1. In a deep-bottom pot, combine lentils, sweet potato, and coconut milk. Get it to a boil.
2. Decrease the stove heat to a simmer and toss in curry powder and turmeric.
3. Cook for 23-25 minutes, stirring occasionally, until the lentils and sweet potato are tender.
4. Adjust seasoning with salt and crushed pepper if needed.
5. Serve warm, and enjoy your rich and flavorful curry!

Prep Time: 10 mins
Cook Time: 25 mins
Serving: 2

NUTRITIONAL VALUES (PER SERVING)

Calories: 300, Protein: 12g, Carbohydrates: 40g, Fat: 10g, Fiber: 8g

SEARED SCALLOPS WITH GARLIC AND SPINACH

INGREDIENTS

- 6 large scallops
- 1 tbsp olive oil
- 1 clove garlic, mashed
- 2 cups fresh spinach
- 1 tsp lemon juice

This elegant Seared Scallops with Garlic and Spinach is a quick and flavorful dinner option, perfect for a light yet satisfying meal.

INSTRUCTIONS

1. Heat one tbsp oil in a skillet over medium-high heat and sear the scallops for 2-3 minutes on one side until golden brown.
2. Remove the scallops and put them aside.
3. Add mashed garlic and sauté for 1 minute.
4. Add spinach and leave until wilted thoroughly for 2 minutes.
5. Return the scallops to the skillet, drizzle one tsp lemon juice, and serve warm. Enjoy!

Prep Time: 5 mins
Cook Time: 10 mins
Serving: 2

NUTRITIONAL VALUES (PER SERVING)

Calories: 220, Protein: 22g, Carbohydrates: 4g, Fat: 12g, Fiber: 2g

TURMERIC CHICKEN STIR-FRY WITH VEGGIES

INGREDIENTS

6 oz chicken breast, diced
1 cup mixed vegetables (e.g., bell peppers, zucchini, carrots)
1 tbsp olive oil
1 tsp ground turmeric
1 tsp soy sauce

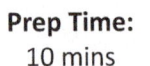

This Turmeric Chicken Stir-Fry with Veggies is a quick and vibrant dinner, combining lean chicken with colorful vegetables and anti-inflammatory turmeric.

INSTRUCTIONS

1. Heat one tbsp oil in a skillet over moderate flame and sauté chicken until golden, about 8 minutes.
2. Add turmeric and mixed vegetables, cooking for 5-7 minutes until tender-crisp.
3. Toss in soy sauce and toss to combine.
4. Cook for more minutes to blend flavors. Serve warm, and enjoy your flavorful stir-fry!

Prep Time: 10 mins
Cook Time: 15 mins
Serving: 2

NUTRITIONAL VALUES (PER SERVING)
Calories: 250, Protein: 28g, Carbohydrates: 8g, Fat: 10g, Fiber: 3g

BAKED EGGPLANT WITH TOMATO SAUCE

INGREDIENTS

1 medium eggplant, sliced into rounds
1 cup canned diced tomatoes
1 tbsp olive oil
1 clove garlic, mashed
1 tsp dried oregano

This Baked Eggplant with Tomato Sauce is a simple yet flavorful dinner that combines tender roasted eggplant with a rich tomato sauce.

INSTRUCTIONS

1. Preheat oven to 375°F (190°C). Brush eggplant pieces with one tbsp oil and arrange on the parchment paper-arranged baking sheet.
2. Roast for 20 minutes, and flip after halftime has passed.
3. In a saucepan, cook diced tomatoes, garlic, and oregano over moderate flame for 5 minutes.
4. Pour the tomato sauce over the roasted eggplant. Serve warm and enjoy this comforting dish!

Prep Time: 10 mins
Cook Time: 25 mins
Serving: 2

NUTRITIONAL VALUES (PER SERVING)

Calories: 180, Protein: 4g, Carbohydrates: 15g, Fat: 12g, Fiber: 5g

SPINACH AND MUSHROOM STUFFED BELL PEPPERS

INGREDIENTS

2 large bell peppers, halved and seeds removed
1 cup fresh spinach, chopped
1 cup mushrooms, diced
1 tbsp olive oil
1 tsp garlic powder

These Spinach and Mushroom Stuffed Bell Peppers are a nutrient-packed dinner option, filled with a savory mixture of spinach and mushrooms baked to perfection.

INSTRUCTIONS

1. Preheat oven to 375°F (190°C). Arrange the bell pepper halves on the parchment paper-arranged baking sheet.
2. Heat one tbsp oil in a skillet over moderate flame and sauté mushrooms and spinach until tender, about 5 minutes.
3. Toss in garlic powder and mix well.
4. Fill each bell pepper in half with the spinach and mushroom mixture.
5. Bake for 20-25 minutes until the peppers are tender. Serve warm and enjoy!

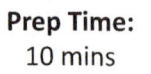

Prep Time: 10 mins
Cook Time: 25 mins
Serving: 2

NUTRITIONAL VALUES (PER SERVING)

Calories: 200, Protein: 6g, Carbohydrates: 15g, Fat: 12g, Fiber: 5g

ROASTED ZUCCHINI AND QUINOA BOWL

INGREDIENTS

1 medium zucchini, sliced
1 cup cooked quinoa
1 tbsp olive oil
1 tsp garlic powder
1 tsp lemon juice

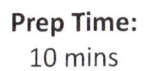

This Roasted Zucchini and Quinoa Bowl is a wholesome, plant-based dinner that combines tender roasted zucchini with protein-rich quinoa for a satisfying and nutritious meal.

INSTRUCTIONS

1. Preheat oven to 400°F (200°C). Toss zucchini slices with olive oil and garlic powder.
2. Arrange zucchini on the parchment paper-arranged baking sheet and roast for 20 minutes; flip after halftime has passed.
3. Divide cooked quinoa between two bowls and top with roasted zucchini.
4. Drizzle one tsp lemon juice and toss gently to combine.
5. Serve warm and enjoy your flavorful, nutrient-rich dinner!

Prep Time: 10 mins
Cook Time: 20 mins
Serving: 2

NUTRITIONAL VALUES (PER SERVING)

Calories: 250, Protein: 8g, Carbohydrates: 35g, Fat: 8g, Fiber: 5g

MISO-GLAZED SALMON WITH BOK CHOY

INGREDIENTS

2 salmon fillets (4-6 oz each)
2 heads bok choy, halved
1 tbsp miso paste
1 tbsp olive oil
1 tsp honey (optional)

This Miso-Glazed Salmon with Bok Choy is a quick and flavorful dinner option. The savory miso glaze enhances the rich flavor of the salmon, while tender bok choy adds freshness to the dish.

INSTRUCTIONS

1. Preheat oven to 375°F (190°C). Mix miso paste, olive oil, and honey to create a glaze.
2. Brush the miso glaze over the fish fillets.
3. Place salmon and bok choy on the parchment paper-arranged baking sheet. Drizzle bok choy with olive oil.
4. Bake for 12-15 minutes until the salmon is done thoroughly and the bok choy is tender.
5. Serve warm, and enjoy your flavorful and healthy meal!

Prep Time: 10 mins
Cook Time: 15 mins
Serving: 2

NUTRITIONAL VALUES (PER SERVING)

Calories: 320, Protein: 28g, Carbohydrates: 5g, Fat: 20g, Fiber: 2g

SWEET POTATO AND KALE STEW

INGREDIENTS

- 1 medium sweet potato, diced
- 2 cups fresh kale, chopped
- 2 cups vegetable broth
- 1 cup canned diced tomatoes
- 1 tsp ground cumin

This hearty Sweet Potato and Kale Stew is a comforting, plant-based dish packed with fiber and antioxidants, making it a perfect anti-inflammatory dinner.

INSTRUCTIONS

1. In a deep-bottom pot, combine diced sweet potato, kale, vegetable broth, and canned tomatoes.
2. Get it to a boil, then reduce to a simmer.
3. Toss in ground cumin and cook for 20-25 minutes until the sweet potato is tender.
4. Adjust seasoning with salt and crushed pepper if needed.
5. Serve warm and enjoy this hearty, nutritious stew!

Prep Time: 10 mins
Cook Time: 25 mins
Serving: 2

NUTRITIONAL VALUES (PER SERVING)

Calories: 240, Protein: 6g, Carbohydrates: 38g, Fat: 6g, Fiber: 8g

BUTTERNUT SQUASH SOUP WITH COCONUT MILK

INGREDIENTS

2 cups butternut squash, diced
1 cup coconut milk
1 cup vegetable broth
1 tsp ground turmeric
1 clove garlic, mashed

This creamy Butternut Squash Soup with Coconut Milk is a warming, anti-inflammatory dish that combines the natural sweetness of squash with the richness of coconut milk.

INSTRUCTIONS

1. In a deep-bottom pot, sauté mashed garlic in a drizzle of olive oil until fragrant.
2. Add butternut squash, vegetable broth, and turmeric. Simmer for 18-20 minutes until squash gets tender.
3. Blend the mixture until smooth in an immersion or regular kitchen blender.
4. Toss in coconut milk and heat through for 2-3 minutes.
5. Serve warm and enjoy your creamy, flavorful soup!

Prep Time: 10 mins
Cook Time: 25 mins
Serving: 2

NUTRITIONAL VALUES (PER SERVING)

Calories: 220, Protein: 3g, Carbohydrates: 28g, Fat: 12g, Fiber: 6g

LEMON THYME CHICKEN WITH ROASTED VEGETABLES

INGREDIENTS

2 chicken breasts
1 cup mixed vegetables (e.g., carrots, zucchini, bell peppers)
1 tbsp olive oil
1 tsp lemon juice
1 tsp fresh thyme

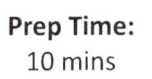

This Lemon Thyme Chicken with Roasted Vegetables is a fragrant and wholesome dinner featuring tender chicken and perfectly roasted veggies infused with fresh thyme and lemon.

INSTRUCTIONS

1. Preheat oven to 375°F (190°C). Toss vegetables with olive oil and arrange on the parchment paper-arranged baking sheet.
2. Season the breast meat with salt, crushed pepper, thyme, and lemon juice. Place on the parchment paper-arranged baking sheet with vegetables.
3. Roast for 20-25 minutes until the chicken is done thoroughly and vegetables are tender.
4. Remove from the oven and let rest for 5 minutes.
5. Serve warm, and enjoy your flavorful, balanced dinner!

Prep Time: 10 mins
Cook Time: 25 mins
Serving: 2

NUTRITIONAL VALUES (PER SERVING)

Calories: 300, Protein: 30g, Carbohydrates: 10g, Fat: 12g, Fiber: 4g

GARLIC GINGER SHRIMP WITH GREEN BEANS

INGREDIENTS

1 cup shrimp, peeled and deveined
1 cup green beans, trimmed
1 tbsp olive oil
1 clove garlic, mashed
1 tsp grated ginger

This Garlic Ginger Shrimp with Green Beans is a quick, flavorful dinner that combines juicy shrimp with crisp green beans in a fragrant garlic-ginger sauce.

INSTRUCTIONS

1. Heat one tbsp oil in a skillet over moderate flame. Add mashed garlic and grated ginger, cooking for 1 minute until fragrant.
2. Add shrimp and sear for 2-3 minutes on one side until pink and fully cooked.
3. Remove shrimp and add green beans to the skillet. Sauté for 3-4 minutes until tender-crisp.
4. Return shrimp and toss with green beans to combine.
5. Serve warm and enjoy this flavorful and protein-packed dish!

Prep Time: 10 mins
Cook Time: 10 mins
Serving: 2

NUTRITIONAL VALUES (PER SERVING)

Calories: 200, Protein: 20g, Carbohydrates: 5g, Fat: 10g, Fiber: 2g

ZUCCHINI NOODLES WITH PESTO AND CHERRY TOMATOES

INGREDIENTS

- 2 medium zucchinis, spiralized
- ½ cup cherry tomatoes, halved
- 2 tbsp pesto
- 1 tbsp olive oil
- 1 tsp lemon juice

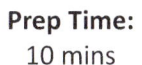

This Zucchini Noodles with Pesto and Cherry Tomatoes is a light, low-carb dinner that's packed with fresh flavors and vibrant colors.

INSTRUCTIONS

1. Heat one tbsp oil in a skillet over moderate flame. Add zucchini noodles and sauté for 2-3 minutes until slightly tender.
2. Remove from heat and toss zucchini noodles with pesto and lemon juice.
3. Add cherry tomatoes and toss softly to combine.
4. Divide between two plates and serve warm or chilled.
5. Enjoy this fresh and healthy dinner option!

Prep Time: 10 mins
Cook Time: 5 mins
Serving: 2

NUTRITIONAL VALUES (PER SERVING)

Calories: 180, Protein: 4g, Carbohydrates: 10g, Fat: 14g, Fiber: 3g

BAKED TROUT WITH DILL AND LEMON

INGREDIENTS

- 2 trout fillets
- 1 tbsp olive oil
- 1 tsp lemon juice
- 1 tsp fresh dill, chopped
- 1 clove garlic, mashed

This Baked Trout with Dill and Lemon is a simple yet elegant dish that highlights the delicate flavor of trout, complemented by the fresh aroma of dill and lemon.

INSTRUCTIONS

1. Preheat oven to 375°F (190°C). Arrange the baking sheet with parchment paper.
2. Place the trout fillets on the parchment paper-arranged baking sheet and drizzle with one tbsp oil and lemon juice.
3. Sprinkle with fresh dill and mashed garlic.
4. Bake for 12-15 minutes until the trout is done thoroughly and flakes easily with a fork.
5. Serve warm, and enjoy this light and flavorful meal!

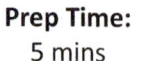

Prep Time: 5 mins
Cook Time: 15 mins
Serving: 2

NUTRITIONAL VALUES (PER SERVING)

Calories: 240, Protein: 25g, Carbohydrates: 2g, Fat: 15g, Fiber: 0g

ROASTED CAULIFLOWER STEAKS WITH TURMERIC SAUCE

INGREDIENTS

1 medium cauliflower sliced into thick steaks
1 tbsp olive oil
1 tsp ground turmeric
1 tsp lemon juice
1 clove garlic, mashed

These Roasted Cauliflower Steaks with Turmeric Sauce are a stunning and flavorful plant-based dinner option, rich in anti-inflammatory properties and vibrant colors.

INSTRUCTIONS

1. Preheat oven to 400°F (200°C). Arrange the baking sheet with parchment paper.
2. Brush cauliflower steaks with olive oil and sprinkle with turmeric.
3. Roast for 20-25 minutes, flip after halftime has passed, until golden and tender.
4. Mix lemon juice and mashed garlic to create a simple sauce, then drizzle over the roasted cauliflower.
5. Serve warm and enjoy your vibrant and flavorful dinner!

Prep Time: 10 mins
Cook Time: 25 mins
Serving: 2

NUTRITIONAL VALUES (PER SERVING)

Calories: 160, Protein: 5g, Carbohydrates: 15g, Fat: 8g, Fiber: 5g

COCONUT CURRY SHRIMP WITH SPINACH

INGREDIENTS

1 cup shrimp, peeled and deveined
2 cups fresh spinach
1 cup coconut milk
1 tsp curry powder
1 tbsp olive oil

This Coconut Curry Shrimp with Spinach is a creamy and fragrant dish, combining tender shrimp with nutrient-rich spinach in a delicious coconut curry sauce.

INSTRUCTIONS

1. Heat one tbsp oil in a skillet over moderate flame and cook shrimp for 2-3 minutes until pink and fully cooked.
2. Remove shrimp and add spinach to the skillet,cooking until wilted, about 2 minutes.
3. Toss in coconut milk and curry powder, mixing well.
4. Return shrimp and simmer for 3-4 minutes to combine flavors.
5. Serve warm, and enjoy this creamy and flavorful dish!

Prep Time: 10 mins
Cook Time: 15 mins
Serving: 2

NUTRITIONAL VALUES (PER SERVING)

Calories: 280, Protein: 20g, Carbohydrates: 6g, Fat: 18g, Fiber: 3g

GRILLED TURKEY BURGERS WITH AVOCADO SALSA

INGREDIENTS

8 oz ground turkey
1 tsp garlic powder
1 tbsp olive oil
1 small avocado, diced
1 medium tomato, diced

These Grilled Turkey Burgers with Avocado Salsa are juicy, flavorful, and packed with lean protein. The creamy avocado salsa adds a fresh and delicious twist to this classic dinner option.

INSTRUCTIONS

1. Mix ground turkey with garlic powder and form into two patties.
2. Heat one tbsp oil in a grill pan over moderate flame and grill the patties for 4-5 minutes on one side until fully cooked.
3. Grab a shallow bowl and combine diced avocado and tomato to make the salsa.
4. Place the turkey burgers on plates and top with the avocado salsa.
5. Serve immediately and enjoy this protein-rich meal!

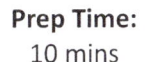

Prep Time: 10 mins
Cook Time: 10 mins
Serving: 2

NUTRITIONAL VALUES (PER SERVING)

Calories: 300, Protein: 25g, Carbohydrates: 6g, Fat: 18g, Fiber: 3g

SPAGHETTI SQUASH WITH BASIL AND GARLIC

INGREDIENTS

1 small spaghetti squash
1 tbsp olive oil
2 cloves garlic, mashed
2 tbsp fresh basil, chopped

This Spaghetti Squash with Basil and Garlic is a low-carb, nutrient-packed alternative to traditional pasta, combining tender spaghetti squash with aromatic basil and garlic.

INSTRUCTIONS

1. Preheat oven to 400°F (200°C). Cut the spaghetti squash in half to discard the seeds.
2. Drizzle one tbsp oil over the squash halves and bake cut-side down for 37-40 minutes until tender.
3. With a fork, scrape out the spaghetti into strands and transfer them to a bowl.
4. In a skillet, sauté mashed garlic in one tbsp oil for 1 minute. Add squash and toss to combine.
5. Spread fresh basil on top and serve warm. Enjoy your flavorful pasta alternative!

Prep Time: 10 mins
Cook Time: 40 mins
Serving: 2

NUTRITIONAL VALUES (PER SERVING)

Calories: 150, Protein: 2g, Carbohydrates: 15g, Fat: 8g, Fiber: 4g

BAKED CHICKEN THIGHS WITH KALE AND SWEET POTATOEAS

INGREDIENTS

2 chicken thighs (bone-in, skin-on)
1 cup sweet potato, diced
2 cups kale, chopped
1 tbsp olive oil
1 tsp paprika

This Baked Chicken Thighs with Kale and Sweet Potatoes is a hearty, one-pan meal that's as delicious as it is nutritious. The sweet potatoes and kale pair perfectly with the tender, flavorful chicken thighs.

INSTRUCTIONS

1. Preheat oven to 375°F (190°C). Arrange the baking sheet with parchment paper.
2. Season the thigh meat with paprika, salt, and crushed pepper.
3. Toss sweet potatoes with one tbsp oil and spread them on the parchment paper-arranged baking sheet. Add chicken thighs.
4. Bake for 25 minutes, then add kale to the baking sheet and bake for more 5 minutes until crispy.
5. Serve warm and enjoy your balanced, flavorful dinner!

Prep Time: 10 mins
Cook Time: 30 mins
Serving: 2

NUTRITIONAL VALUES (PER SERVING)

Calories: 350, Protein: 25g, Carbohydrates: 18g, Fat: 20g, Fiber: 4g

LENTIL STEW WITH GARLIC AND ROSEMARY

INGREDIENTS

- ½ cup dried lentils
- 2 cups vegetable broth
- 1 clove garlic, mashed
- 1 tsp fresh rosemary, chopped
- 1 cup diced tomatoes

This comforting Lentil Stew with Garlic and Rosemary is packed with earthy flavors and plant-based protein, making it a hearty and satisfying dinner choice.

INSTRUCTIONS

1. In a deep-bottom pot, combine lentils, vegetable broth, and diced tomatoes. Get it to a boil.
2. Decrease the stove heat and add mashed garlic and rosemary. Simmer for 23-25 minutes until tender.
3. Adjust seasoning with salt and crushed pepper if needed.
4. Divide into bowls and spread additional rosemary on top if desired.
5. Serve warm, and enjoy this hearty, flavorful stew!

Prep Time: 10 mins
Cook Time: 25 mins
Serving: 2

NUTRITIONAL VALUES (PER SERVING)

Calories: 250, Protein: 12g, Carbohydrates: 35g, Fat: 4g, Fiber: 9g

ROASTED BRUSSELS SPROUTS AND CHICKPEA BOWL

INGREDIENTS

1 cup Brussels sprouts, halved
1 cup cooked chickpeas
1 tbsp olive oil
1 tsp smoked paprika
1 tsp lemon juice

This Roasted Brussels Sprouts and Chickpea Bowl is a nutrient-dense, plant-based meal that's perfect for a light yet satisfying dinner.

INSTRUCTIONS

1. Preheat oven to 400°F (200°C). Arrange the baking sheet with parchment paper.
2. Toss the Brussels sprouts and chickpeas with one tbsp oil and smoked paprika. Spread evenly on the parchment paper-arranged baking sheet.
3. Roast for 20 minutes, flip after halftime has passed, until golden and tender.
4. Divide into bowls and drizzle one tsp lemon juice.
5. Serve warm and enjoy this flavorful, plant-based meal!

Prep Time: 10 mins
Cook Time: 20 mins
Serving: 2

NUTRITIONAL VALUES (PER SERVING)

Calories: 220, Protein: 8g, Carbohydrates: 28g, Fat: 8g, Fiber: 7g

SNACKS

CUCUMBER SLICES WITH TURMERIC HUMMUS

INGREDIENTS

1 medium cucumber, sliced
½ cup hummus
½ tsp ground turmeric
1 tsp lemon juice
1 tsp olive oil

This Cucumber Slices with Turmeric Hummus is a refreshing and nutritious snack, perfect for quick bites. The creamy hummus, infused with turmeric, pairs perfectly with crisp cucumber slices.

INSTRUCTIONS

1. Grab a shallow bowl and mix hummus with turmeric, lemon juice, and olive oil until well combined.
2. Arrange cucumber slices on a plate. Spoon the turmeric hummus into a serving bowl.
3. Serve the cucumber slices alongside the hummus.
4. Dip and enjoy this vibrant and healthy snack!

Prep Time: 10 mins
Cook Time: 00 mins
Serving: 2

NUTRITIONAL VALUES (PER SERVING)

Calories: 150, Protein: 5g, Carbohydrates: 12g, Fat: 8g, Fiber: 3g

MIXED BERRY AND WALNUT ENERGY BITES

INGREDIENTS

½ cup mixed dried berries
½ cup walnuts
2 tbsp almond butter
1 tbsp chia seeds
1 tsp honey (optional)

These Mixed Berry and Walnut Energy Bites are naturally sweetened and packed with energy-boosting ingredients, making them perfect for on-the-go snacking.

INSTRUCTIONS

1. In a food blender, combine dried berries, walnuts, almond butter, and chia seeds.
2. Pulse until the mixture until the texture forms a sticky dough. Add honey if desired for extra sweetness.
3. Roll the mixture into small, bite-sized balls.
4. Refrigerate for 30 minutes to set. Serve chilled and enjoy!

Prep Time: 10 mins
Cook Time: 00 mins
Serving: 2

NUTRITIONAL VALUES (PER SERVING)

Calories: 180, Protein: 4g, Carbohydrates: 15g, Fat: 12g, Fiber: 4g

CARROT STICKS WITH LEMON TAHINI DIP

INGREDIENTS

2 medium carrots, cut into sticks
2 tbsp tahini
1 tsp lemon juice
1 clove garlic, mashed
1 tbsp water

This Carrot Sticks with Lemon Tahini Dip is a crunchy and creamy snack packed with vitamins and healthy fats. It's an easy and flavorful way to enjoy your veggies.

INSTRUCTIONS

1. Take a small shallow bowl and mix tahini, lemon juice, mashed garlic, and water until smooth.
2. Arrange carrot sticks on a plate. Spoon the lemon tahini dip into a serving bowl.
3. Serve the dip alongside the carrot sticks. Dip and enjoy your healthy snack!

Prep Time: 10 mins
Cook Time: 00 mins
Serving: 2

NUTRITIONAL VALUES (PER SERVING)

Calories: 120, Protein: 3g, Carbohydrates: 12g, Fat: 6g, Fiber: 4g

COCONUT AND MATCHA BLISS BALLS

INGREDIENTS

½ cup shredded coconut
1 tbsp matcha powder
2 tbsp almond butter
1 tsp honey (optional)
1 tbsp chia seeds

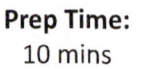

These Coconut and Matcha Bliss Balls are energizing, nutrient-dense bites infused with the earthy flavor of matcha and the sweetness of coconut. Perfect for a quick snack or dessert!

INSTRUCTIONS

1. Grab a shallow bowl and mix shredded coconut, matcha powder, almond butter, honey, and chia seeds until combined.
2. Roll the mixture into small balls. Refrigerate for 30 minutes to set.
3. Serve chilled or at room temperature. Enjoy these delicious, energy-boosting bliss balls!

Prep Time: 10 mins
Cook Time: 00 mins
Serving: 2

NUTRITIONAL VALUES (PER SERVING)

Calories: 150, Protein: 3g, Carbohydrates: 10g, Fat: 11g, Fiber: 3g

DARK CHOCOLATE DIPPED STRAWBERRIES

INGREDIENTS

1 cup fresh strawberries
½ cup dark chocolate chips
1 tsp coconut oil

These Dark Chocolate Dipped Strawberries are a simple and elegant snack or dessert, combining the sweetness of fresh strawberries with dark chocolate richness.

INSTRUCTIONS

1. Melt dark chocolate chips with one tsp coconut oil, heating in 20-second intervals and stirring until smooth.
2. Dip every strawberry into the melted chocolate, coating it halfway.
3. Spread the chocolate dipped strawberries on a parchment paper-arranged tray.
4. Refrigerate for 12 minutes until the chocolate hardens.
5. Serve and enjoy this indulgent yet healthy treat!

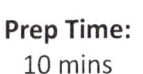

Prep Time: 10 mins
Cook Time: 5 mins
Serving: 2

NUTRITIONAL VALUES (PER SERVING)

Calories: 120, Protein: 2g, Carbohydrates: 15g, Fat: 7g, Fiber: 3g

SLICED PEAR WITH WALNUT AND HONEY DRIZZLE

INGREDIENTS

1 ripe pear, thinly sliced
2 tbsp chopped walnuts
1 tsp honey

This Sliced Pear with Walnut and Honey Drizzle is a simple yet delightful snack, combining the natural sweetness of pears with the crunch of walnuts and a touch of honey.

INSTRUCTIONS

1. Arrange the pear slices on a serving plate. Sprinkle chopped walnuts evenly over the pear slices.
2. Drizzle honey over the pears and walnuts. Serve immediately and enjoy this naturally sweet snack!

Prep Time: 5 mins
Cook Time: 00 mins
Serving: 2

NUTRITIONAL VALUES (PER SERVING)
Calories: 120, Protein: 2g, Carbohydrates: 20g, Fat: 4g, Fiber: 4g

PUMPKIN SEEDS WITH CHILI POWDER

INGREDIENTS

½ cup raw pumpkin seeds
1 tsp olive oil
½ tsp chili powder

These Pumpkin Seeds with Chili Powder are a quick and spicy snack packed with crunch and nutrients. Perfect for on-the-go snacking or as a savory treat.

INSTRUCTIONS

1. Preheat a skillet over moderate flame and add olive oil.
2. Toss pumpkin seeds with chili powder and add to the skillet.
3. Toast the seeds for 5-7 minutes, stirring frequently, until golden and fragrant.
4. Remove from heat and let cool slightly.
5. Serve and enjoy this spicy, crunchy snack!

Prep Time: 5 mins
Cook Time: 10 mins
Serving: 2

NUTRITIONAL VALUES (PER SERVING)

Calories: 120, Protein: 6g, Carbohydrates: 3g, Fat: 10g, Fiber: 2g

AVOCADO AND TOMATO MINI TOASTS

INGREDIENTS

2 slices whole-grain bread, cut into halves
1 small avocado, mashed
1 small tomato, diced
1 tsp olive oil

These Avocado and Tomato Mini toast are a quick and nutritious snack that combines creamy avocado with juicy tomatoes for a delightful burst of flavor.

INSTRUCTIONS

1. Toast the whole-grain bread slices to your preferred level of crispiness.
2. Spread mashed avocado evenly on each piece of toast.
3. Top with diced tomato and drizzle with one tsp oil.
4. Sprinkle with salt and crushed pepper if desired.
5. Serve immediately and enjoy!

Prep Time: 5 mins
Cook Time: 00 mins
Serving: 2

NUTRITIONAL VALUES (PER SERVING)

Calories: 150, Protein: 4g, Carbohydrates: 18g, Fat: 8g, Fiber: 4g

MANGO AND ALMOND BUTTER ROLL-UPS

INGREDIENTS

1 medium ripe mango, thinly sliced
2 tbsp almond butter
1 tsp shredded coconut

These Mango and Almond Butter Roll-Ups are a fun and refreshing snack that combines the sweetness of mango with the creamy richness of almond butter.

INSTRUCTIONS

1. Lay mango slices flat on a plate.
2. Spread almond butter (a thin layer) on each slice.
3. Sprinkle with shredded coconut.
4. Roll the mango slices tightly and secure with toothpicks if needed.
5. Serve immediately and enjoy this sweet and satisfying snack!

Prep Time: 5 mins
Cook Time: 00 mins
Serving: 2

NUTRITIONAL VALUES (PER SERVING)

Calories: 140, Protein: 3g, Carbohydrates: 20g, Fat: 6g, Fiber: 3g

BAKED ZUCCHINI CHIPS

INGREDIENTS

1 medium zucchini, thinly sliced
1 tbsp olive oil
½ tsp paprika

These Baked Zucchini Chips are a crunchy, healthy snack alternative to traditional
chips, seasoned with a touch of olive oil and spices.

INSTRUCTIONS

1. Preheat oven to 375°F (190°C). Arrange the baking sheet with parchment paper.
2. Toss zucchini slices with olive oil and paprika in a bowl.
3. Arrange the slices in a single layer on the parchment paper-arranged baking sheet.
4. Bake for 20 minutes, flip after halftime has passed, until crispy and golden.
5. Serve and enjoy your healthy, crunchy snack!

Prep Time: 10 mins
Cook Time: 20 mins
Serving: 2

NUTRITIONAL VALUES (PER SERVING)

Calories: 100, Protein: 2g, Carbohydrates: 5g, Fat: 8g, Fiber: 2g

CUCUMBER AND DILL YOGURT DIP

INGREDIENTS

1 cup unsweetened Greek yogurt
½ cup cucumber, grated
1 tsp fresh dill, chopped
1 tsp lemon juice
1 clove garlic, mashed

This Cucumber and Dill Yogurt Dip is a refreshing and creamy snack that pairs perfectly with crackers or fresh veggies. It's light, flavorful, and packed with anti-inflammatory

INSTRUCTIONS

1. Grab a shallow bowl and mix Greek yogurt, grated cucumber, dill, lemon juice, and garlic until well combined.
2. Powder it with salt and crushed pepper if desired.
3. Chill in the refrigerator for 10 minutes to enhance flavors.
4. Serve with crackers and veggie sticks.
5. Enjoy this light and refreshing dip!

Prep Time: 5 mins
Cook Time: 00 mins
Serving: 2

NUTRITIONAL VALUES (PER SERVING)

Calories: 80, Protein: 6g, Carbohydrates: 5g, Fat: 3g, Fiber: 1g

SWEET POTATO ROUNDS WITH HUMMUS

INGREDIENTS

1 medium sweet potato, sliced into rounds
1 tbsp olive oil
½ cup hummus
1 tsp paprika

These Sweet Potato Rounds with Hummus are a nutrient-dense snack that combines the sweetness of roasted sweet potato with the creaminess of hummus for a delightful bite.

INSTRUCTIONS

1. Preheat oven to 400°F (200°C). Arrange the baking sheet with parchment paper.
2. Toss sweet potato wedges with one tbsp oil and arrange them on the parchment paper-arranged baking sheet.
3. Roast for 20 minutes, flip after halftime has passed until tender and lightly crisped.
4. Top each round with a dollop of hummus and sprinkle with paprika.
5. Serve warm and enjoy!

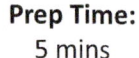

Prep Time: 5 mins
Cook Time: 20 mins
Serving: 2

NUTRITIONAL VALUES (PER SERVING)

Calories: 150, Protein: 4g, Carbohydrates: 20g, Fat: 6g, Fiber: 4g

FRESH PINEAPPLE WITH COCONUT FLAKES

INGREDIENTS

1 cup fresh pineapple
2 tbsp unsweetened coconut flakes

This Fresh Pineapple with Coconut Flakes is a tropical-inspired snack that's simple, refreshing, and naturally sweet. Perfect for a quick, healthy treatment!

INSTRUCTIONS

1. With the shapr knife and cut the pineapple in to cubes. Arrange pineapple cubes on a serving plate.
2. Sprinkle with unsweetened coconut flakes.
3. Serve immediately and enjoy this tropical delight!

Prep Time: 5 mins
Cook Time: 00 mins
Serving: 2

NUTRITIONAL VALUES (PER SERVING)

Calories: 90, Protein: 1g, Carbohydrates: 20g, Fat: 2g, Fiber: 2g

RAW VEGGIE STICKS WITH CASHEW DIP

INGREDIENTS

1 cup mixed veggie sticks (carrots, celery, bell peppers)
½ cup cashews, soaked and drained
1 tsp lemon juice
1 clove garlic
2 tbsp water

These Raw Veggie Sticks with Cashew Dip make for a crunchy and creamy snack that's packed with nutrients. It's perfect for dipping and sharing!

INSTRUCTIONS

1. Blend soaked cashews, lemon juice, garlic, and water in a food blender until smooth.
2. Adjust the consistency by adding more water if needed.
3. Arrange the veggie sticks on a serving plate.
4. Spoon the cashew dip into a small bowl.
5. Serve and enjoy this healthy and satisfying snack!

Prep Time: 10 mins
Cook Time: 00 mins
Serving: 2

NUTRITIONAL VALUES (PER SERVING)

Calories: 160, Protein: 5g, Carbohydrates: 12g, Fat: 10g, Fiber: 3g

CINNAMON ROASTED APPLES

INGREDIENTS

2 medium apples, sliced
1 tbsp coconut oil
1 tsp ground cinnamon

These Cinnamon Roasted Apples are a warm and comforting snack or dessert that combines the natural sweetness of apples with the aromatic spice of cinnamon.

INSTRUCTIONS

1. Preheat oven to 375°F (190°C). Arrange the baking sheet with parchment paper.
2. Toss the apple slices with melted one tsp coconut oil and cinnamon.
3. Spread the slices evenly on the parchment paper-arranged baking sheet.
4. Roast for 15 minutes, flip after halftime has passed, until tender and fragrant.
5. Serve warm and enjoy this cozy, spiced treat!

Prep Time: 5 mins
Cook Time: 15 mins
Serving: 2

NUTRITIONAL VALUES (PER SERVING)

Calories: 120, Protein: 0g, Carbohydrates: 25g, Fat: 4g, Fiber: 4g

DESSERTS

DARK CHOCOLATE AVOCADO MOUSSE

INGREDIENTS

1 ripe avocado
2 tbsp unsweetened cocoa powder
2 tbsp maple syrup
2 tbsp almond milk
½ tsp vanilla extract

This Dark Chocolate Avocado Mousse is a rich, creamy dessert packed with healthy fats and antioxidants. It's a guilt-free indulgence for chocolate lovers.

INSTRUCTIONS

1. In a food blender, combine avocado, cocoa powder, maple syrup, almond milk, and vanilla extract.
2. Blend on full power until the texture turns smooth and creamy. Adjust sweetness if needed.
3. Divide the mousse into the wide-mouth serving bowls or glasses.
4. Chill for 30 minutes before serving.
5. Spread fresh berries or a sprinkle of cocoa powder, and enjoy!

Prep Time: 10 mins
Cook Time: 00 mins
Serving: 2

NUTRITIONAL VALUES (PER SERVING)

Calories: 180, Protein: 2g, Carbohydrates: 18g, Fat: 12g, Fiber: 5g

RASPBERRY AND ALMOND FLOUR CRUMBLE

INGREDIENTS

- 1 cup fresh raspberries
- ¼ cup almond flour
- 1 tbsp coconut oil, melted
- 1 tsp honey
- ½ tsp cinnamon

This Raspberry and Almond Flour Crumble is a light and fruity dessert with a crunchy almond topping, perfect for a quick and healthy treat.

INSTRUCTIONS

1. Preheat oven to 375°F (190°C). Grease a small baking dish.
2. Spread raspberries evenly in the dish.
3. Grab a shallow bowl and mix almond flour, melted coconut oil, honey, and cinnamon until crumbly.
4. Sprinkle the crumble mixture over the raspberries.
5. Bake for 17-20 minutes until the topping turns golden. Serve warm and enjoy!

Prep Time: 10 mins
Cook Time: 20 mins
Serving: 2

NUTRITIONAL VALUES (PER SERVING)

Calories: 140, Protein: 3g, Carbohydrates: 12g, Fat: 9g, Fiber: 4g

MATCHA GREEN TEA COCONUT BALLS

INGREDIENTS

½ cup shredded coconut
1 tbsp matcha powder
2 tbsp almond butter
1 tsp maple syrup
1 tbsp chia seeds

These Matcha Green Tea Coconut Balls are energizing and packed with antioxidants, making them a perfect bite-sized dessert or snack.

INSTRUCTIONS

1. Grab a shallow bowl and mix shredded coconut, matcha powder, almond butter, maple syrup, and chia seeds until combined.
2. Roll the mixture into small balls.
3. Refrigerate for 30 minutes to set.
4. Serve chilled and enjoy these antioxidant-packed treats!

Prep Time: 10 mins
Cook Time: 00 mins
Serving: 2

NUTRITIONAL VALUES (PER SERVING)

Calories: 150, Protein: 3g, Carbohydrates: 10g, Fat: 11g, Fiber: 3g

ANTI-INFLAMMATORY TURMERIC LATTE ICE CREAM

INGREDIENTS

1 cup coconut milk
1 tsp ground turmeric
½ tsp ground cinnamon
1 tbsp honey
½ tsp vanilla extract

This Anti-Inflammatory Turmeric Latte Ice Cream combines the warm flavors of turmeric and cinnamon with the coconut milk creaminess for a refreshing and health-boosting dessert.

INSTRUCTIONS

1. In a blender, combine coconut milk, turmeric, cinnamon, honey, and vanilla extract. Blend on full power until the texture turns smooth.
2. Pour the mixture into a freezer-safe container.
3. Freeze for 4 hours (at least), stirring every hour for a smoother texture.
4. Scoop into bowls and serve.
5. Enjoy this creamy, anti-inflammatory treat!

Prep Time: 10 mins
Cook Time: 00 mins
Serving: 2

NUTRITIONAL VALUES (PER SERVING)

Calories: 140, Protein: 1g, Carbohydrates: 15g, Fat: 9g, Fiber: 1g

LEMON AND BLUEBERRY COCONUT TART

INGREDIENTS

- ½ cup shredded coconut
- 2 tbsp almond flour
- 1 tbsp coconut oil, melted
- 2 tbsp fresh lemon juice
- ¼ cup fresh blueberries

This Lemon and Blueberry Coconut Tart is a refreshing and zesty dessert with a coconut base and a luscious lemon filling topped with fresh blueberries.

INSTRUCTIONS

1. Preheat oven to 350°F (175°C). Mix shredded coconut, almond flour, and melted coconut oil in a bowl to form the crust.
2. Press the mixture into two small tart pans or ramekins. Bake for 8-10 minutes until golden.
3. Grab a shallow bowl and mix lemon juice with honey (optional) for the filling.
4. Pour the lemon mixture over the cooled crusts and top with fresh blueberries.
5. Chill for 15 minutes before serving. Enjoy this tangy, delightful dessert!

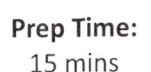

Prep Time: 15 mins
Cook Time: 10 mins
Serving: 2

NUTRITIONAL VALUES (PER SERVING)

Calories: 170, Protein: 3g, Carbohydrates: 14g, Fat: 11g, Fiber: 3g

SWEET POTATO BROWNIES

INGREDIENTS

½ cup mashed sweet potato
2 tbsp almond flour
2 tbsp unsweetened cocoa powder
1 tbsp maple syrup
1 tsp vanilla extract

These Sweet Potato Brownies are a decadent and guilt-free dessert, combining the natural sweetness of sweet potatoes with the richness of cocoa powder for a moist, fudgy treat.

INSTRUCTIONS

1. Preheat oven to 350°F (175°C). Grease a small baking dish.
2. Grab a shallow bowl and combine mashed sweet potato, almond flour, cocoa powder, maple syrup, and vanilla extract. Mix until smooth.
3. Ladle batter into the prepared baking dish and spread evenly.
4. Bake for 25 minutes until set. Let cool before slicing.
5. Serve and enjoy your rich, fudgy brownies!

Prep Time: 10 mins
Cook Time: 25 mins
Serving: 2

NUTRITIONAL VALUES (PER SERVING)

Calories: 160, Protein: 3g, Carbohydrates: 20g, Fat: 7g, Fiber: 4g

ORANGE AND GINGER SORBET

INGREDIENTS

1 cup fresh orange juice
1 tsp grated ginger
1 tbsp honey (optional)

This Orange and Ginger Sorbet is a refreshing and zesty dessert, combining the citrusy sweetness of oranges with the warmth of ginger for a perfect summer treat.

INSTRUCTIONS

1. In a blender, combine orange juice, grated ginger, and honey (if using). Blend on full power until the texture turns smooth.
2. Pour the mixture into a freezer-safe container.
3. Freeze for 3 hours, stirring every hour to prevent ice crystals.
4. Scoop into bowls and serve.
5. Enjoy this refreshing and light dessert!

Prep Time: 10 mins
Cook Time: 00 mins
Serving: 2

NUTRITIONAL VALUES (PER SERVING)

Calories: 80, Protein: 1g, Carbohydrates: 18g, Fat: 0g, Fiber: 1g

BANANA AND TURMERIC ICE CREAM

INGREDIENTS

2 ripe bananas, sliced and frozen
1 tsp ground turmeric
1 tbsp almond milk
½ tsp vanilla extract

This creamy Banana and Turmeric Ice Cream is a healthy, anti-inflammatory dessert that's naturally sweetened with ripe bananas and spiced with turmeric.

INSTRUCTIONS

1. In a blender, combine frozen banana slices, turmeric, almond milk, and vanilla extract. Blend on full power until the texture turns smooth.
2. Transfer the mixture to a freezer-safe container.
3. Freeze for 3 hours, stirring halfway through.
4. Scoop into bowls and serve.
5. Enjoy this creamy, flavorful ice cream!

Prep Time: 5 mins
Cook Time: 00 mins
Serving: 2

NUTRITIONAL VALUES (PER SERVING)

Calories: 120, Protein: 1g, Carbohydrates: 30g, Fat: 0g, Fiber: 3g

GINGER AND LEMON CAKE BITES

INGREDIENTS

- ½ cup almond flour
- 1 tbsp fresh lemon juice
- 1 tsp grated ginger
- 1 tbsp honey
- ½ tsp baking powder

These Ginger and Lemon Cake Bites are soft, zesty, and packed with warming ginger flavor. Perfect as a light dessert or snack!

INSTRUCTIONS

1. Preheat oven to 350°F (175°C). Grease a mini muffin tin or baking dish.
2. Grab a shallow bowl and mix almond flour, lemon juice, grated ginger, honey, and baking powder until combined.
3. Ladle batter into the mini muffin tin or form small balls and place on the parchment paper-arranged baking sheet.
4. Bake for 12-15 minutes until golden.
5. Cool slightly, and enjoy these soft, zesty cake bites!

Prep Time: 10 mins
Cook Time: 15 mins
Serving: 2

NUTRITIONAL VALUES (PER SERVING)

Calories: 120, Protein: 3g, Carbohydrates: 8g, Fat: 8g, Fiber: 2g

PUMPKIN AND COCONUT CREAM MOUSSE

INGREDIENTS

- ½ cup pumpkin puree
- ½ cup coconut cream
- 1 tbsp maple syrup
- ½ tsp ground cinnamon
- ½ tsp vanilla extract

This Pumpkin and Coconut Cream Mousse is a rich and creamy dessert that combines the earthy sweetness of pumpkin with the richness of coconut cream for a delightful fall treat.

INSTRUCTIONS

1. Grab a shallow bowl and toss pumpkin puree, coconut cream, maple syrup, cinnamon, and vanilla extract until smooth.
2. Ladle mixture into serving glasses or wide-mouth bowls.
3. Chill in the refrigerator for at least 30 minutes before serving.
4. Spread a sprinkle of cinnamon or shredded coconut if desired.
5. Serve and enjoy this creamy and spiced dessert!

Prep Time: 10 mins
Cook Time: 00 mins
Serving: 2

NUTRITIONAL VALUES (PER SERVING)

Calories: 150, Protein: 1g, Carbohydrates: 10g, Fat: 12g, Fiber: 3g

SHOPPING LIST

30 DAYS MEAL PLAN

WEEK 1

Produce:
- Spinach (4 cups)
- Kale (3 bunches)
- Sweet potatoes (6 medium)
- Broccoli (1 head)
- Zucchini (3)
- Cherry tomatoes (1 pint)
- Avocados (6)
- Green apple (2)
- Pear (2)
- Banana (2)
- Lemons (4)
- Garlic (3 cloves)
- Ginger (1 knob)
- Onion (1)
- Mushrooms (1 cup)

Grains & Legumes:
- Quinoa (2 cups)
- Rolled oats (1 cup)
- Almond flour (½ cup)
- Chickpeas (1 can or 1 cup dried)
- Lentils (1½ cups dried)

Protein:
- Salmon fillets (3)
- Chicken breast (3 pieces)
- Eggs (1 dozen)
- Dairy & Alternatives:
- Coconut yogurt (1 cup)
- Almond milk (1 quart)

Pantry Items:
- Olive oil (1 bottle)
- Turmeric powder
- Ground cinnamon
- Tahini (½ cup)

WEEK 2

Produce:
- Spinach (4 cups)
- Kale (3 bunches)
- Sweet potatoes (4)
- Zucchini (3)
- Bok choy (1 head)
- Butternut squash (1 small)
- Avocados (5)
- Blueberries (1 pint)
- Raspberries (½ pint)
- Bananas (2)
- Lemons (4)
- Garlic (2 cloves)
- Ginger (1 knob)
- Cherry tomatoes (1 pint)
- Cucumber (2)

Grains & Legumes:
- Quinoa (1½ cups)
- Brown rice (½ cup)
- Lentils (1 cup dried)
- Almond flour (½ cup)

Protein:
- Salmon fillets (3)
- Chicken thighs (4 pieces)
- Eggs (1 dozen)
- Dairy & Alternatives:
- Coconut milk (1 can)
- Almond milk (1 quart)

Pantry Items:
- Olive oil (1 bottle)
- Turmeric powder
- Ground cinnamon
- Matcha powder

SHOPPING LIST

WEEK 3

Produce:
Spinach (4 cups)
Kale (3 bunches)
Sweet potatoes (4)
Zucchini (4)
Avocados (5)
Ginger (1 knob)
Garlic (3 cloves)
Mushrooms (1 cup)
Cucumber (2)
Cherry tomatoes (1 pint)
Raspberries (½ pint)
Blueberries (1 pint)
Lemons (4)
Pear (2)

Grains & Legumes:
Quinoa (1½ cups)
Lentils (1½ cups dried)
Rolled oats (1 cup)

Protein:
Salmon fillets (3)
Chicken thighs (3 pieces)
Eggs (1 dozen)

Dairy & Alternatives:
Coconut yogurt (1 cup)
Coconut milk (1 can)
Almond milk (1 quart)

Pantry Items:
Olive oil (1 bottle)
Turmeric powder
Ground cinnamon
Matcha powder

WEEK 4

Produce:
Spinach (4 cups)
Kale (2 bunches)
Sweet potatoes (5)
Zucchini (3)
Avocados (6)
Mangoes (2)
Pineapple (1 small)
Apples (2)
Lemons (4)
Garlic (3 cloves)
Ginger (1 knob)
Mushrooms (1 cup)
Cucumber (1)
Cherry tomatoes (1 pint)

Grains & Legumes:
Quinoa (1 cup)
Rolled oats (1 cup)
Almond flour (½ cup)
Lentils (1½ cups dried)

Protein:
Trout fillets (2)
Shrimp (1 pound)
Chicken breast (3 pieces)
Eggs (1 dozen)

Dairy & Alternatives:
Coconut milk (1 can)
Almond milk (1 quart)

Pantry Items:
Olive oil (1 bottle)
Turmeric powder
Ground cinnamon
Cashew butter (½ cup)

1ST WEEK MEAL PLAN

DAY 1

Breakfast: Turmeric Spiced Smoothie Bowl

Lunch: Grilled Salmon with Quinoa and Spinach

Dinner: Baked Cod with Tomato and Basil Sauce

Snack: Cucumber Slices with Turmeric Hummus

DAY 2

Breakfast: Avocado and Spinach Omelet

Lunch: Roasted Vegetable and Chickpea Bowl

Dinner: Ginger Sesame Shrimp Stir-Fry with Zucchini

Dessert: Dark Chocolate Avocado Mousse

DAY 3

Breakfast: Sweet Potato and Kale Hash with Poached Egg

Lunch: Turkey and Avocado Lettuce Wraps

Dinner: Lentil Curry with Sweet Potatoes

Snack: Mixed Berry and Walnut Energy Bites

DAY 4

Breakfast: Anti-Inflammatory Golden Milk Oats

Lunch: Chicken Salad with Olive Oil Dressing

Dinner: Turmeric-Spiced Roasted Cauliflower and Tofu

Dessert: Raspberry and Almond Flour Crumble

DAY 5

Breakfast: Green Apple and Almond Butter Toast

Lunch: Spicy Quinoa Salad with Kale and Nuts

Dinner: Salmon with Dill and Lemon Sauce

Snack: Carrot Sticks with Lemon Tahini Dip

DAY 6

Breakfast: Quinoa Breakfast Bowl with Almonds

Lunch: Grilled Chicken with Zucchini Noodles

Dinner: Seared Scallops with Garlic and Spinach

Dessert: Matcha Green Tea Coconut Balls

DAY 7

Breakfast: Banana and Walnut Chia Pudding

Lunch: Avocado and Cucumber Sushi Rolls

Dinner: Spinach and Mushroom Stuffed Bell Peppers

Snack: Dark Chocolate Dipped Strawberries

2ND WEEK MEAL PLAN

DAY 1

Breakfast: Coconut Yogurt with Berries and Seeds

Lunch: Sweet Potato and Lentil Curry

Dinner: Roasted Zucchini and Quinoa Bowl

Dessert: Anti-Inflammatory Turmeric Latte Ice Cream

DAY 2

Breakfast: Lemon Turmeric Overnight Oats

Lunch: Salmon and Cucumber Salad

Dinner: Miso-Glazed Salmon with Bok Choy

Snack: Sliced Pear with Walnut and Honey Drizzle

DAY 3

Breakfast: Sweet Potato Pancakes with Cinnamon

Lunch: Turmeric Chickpea Buddha Bowl

Dinner: Sweet Potato and Kale Stew

Dessert: Lemon and Blueberry Coconut Tart

DAY 4

Breakfast: Apple and Almond Butter Wrap

Lunch: Baked Falafel with Tahini Drizzle

Dinner: Roasted Brussels Sprouts and Chickpea Bowl

Snack: Pumpkin Seeds with Chili Powder

DAY 5

Breakfast: Turmeric and Ginger Infused Porridge

Lunch: Warm Beet and Spinach Salad

Dinner: Butternut Squash Soup with Coconut Milk

Dessert: Sweet Potato Brownies

DAY 6

Breakfast: Avocado and Tomato Whole Grain Toast

Lunch: Tomato and Avocado Gazpacho

Dinner: Lemon Thyme Chicken with Roasted Vegetables

Snack: Avocado and Tomato Mini Toasts

DAY 7

Breakfast: Spiced Pear and Oat Parfait

Lunch: Lemon Herb Shrimp Salad

Dinner: Garlic Ginger Shrimp with Green Beans

Dessert: Orange and Ginger Sorbet

3RD WEEK MEAL PLAN

DAY 1

Breakfast: Spinach and Mushroom Egg Muffins

Lunch: Cauliflower Rice Stir-Fry with Tofu

Dinner: Zucchini Noodles with Pesto and Cherry Tomatoes

Snack: Mango and Almond Butter Roll-Ups

DAY 2

Breakfast: Mango and Coconut Chia Pudding

Lunch: Coconut Curry Lentil Soup

Dinner: Baked Trout with Dill and Lemon

Dessert: Banana and Turmeric Ice Cream

DAY 3

Breakfast: Lemon and Flaxseed Protein Pancakes

Lunch: Roasted Squash and Quinoa Salad

Dinner: Roasted Cauliflower Steaks with Turmeric Sauce

Snack: Baked Zucchini Chips

DAY 4

Breakfast: Matcha Green Tea Smoothie

Lunch: Grilled Eggplant and Chickpea Wraps

Dinner: Coconut Curry Shrimp with Spinach

Dessert: Ginger and Lemon Cake Bites

DAY 5

Breakfast: Golden Milk Breakfast Bowl

Lunch: Ginger Lime Shrimp Bowls

Dinner: Grilled Turkey Burgers with Avocado Salsa

Snack: Cucumber and Dill Yogurt Dip

DAY 6

Breakfast: Raspberry and Almond Oatmeal

Lunch: Grilled Turkey Patties with Cucumber Salad

Dinner: Spaghetti Squash with Basil and Garlic

Dessert: Pumpkin and Coconut Cream Mousse

DAY 7

Breakfast: Ginger and Apple Spiced Smoothie
Lunch: Steamed Veggie with Sesame Dressing
Dinner: Lentil Stew with Garlic and Rosemary
Snack: Sweet Potato Rounds with Hummus

4TH WEEK MEAL PLAN

DAY 1

Breakfast: Turmeric Scrambled Eggs with Spinach

Lunch: Spicy Lentil and Tomato Soup

Dinner: Baked Chicken Thighs with Kale and Sweet Potatoes

Dessert: Dark Chocolate Avocado Mousse

DAY 2

Breakfast: Roasted Sweet Potato and Avocado Mash

Lunch: Zucchini and Sweet Potato Fritters

Dinner: Roasted Veggie Wraps with Hummus

Snack: Fresh Pineapple with Coconut Flakes

DAY 3

Breakfast: Greek-Inspired Egg Wraps

Lunch: Ginger Chicken and Brown Rice Bowl

Dinner: Salmon with Dill and Lemon Sauce

Dessert: Lemon and Blueberry Coconut Tart

DAY 4

Breakfast: Cinnamon and Pumpkin Breakfast Porridge

Lunch: Spicy Quinoa Salad with Kale and Nuts

Dinner: Seared Scallops with Garlic and Spinach

Snack: Raw Veggie Sticks with Cashew Dip

DAY 5

Breakfast: Matcha Green Tea Smoothie

Lunch: Roasted Vegetable and Chickpea Bowl

Dinner: Coconut Curry Shrimp with Spinach

Dessert: Sweet Potato Brownies

DAY 6

Breakfast: Turmeric Spiced Smoothie Bowl

Lunch: Salmon and Cucumber Salad

Dinner: Garlic Ginger Shrimp with Green Beans

Snack: Cucumber Slices with Turmeric Hummus

DAY 7

Breakfast: Golden Milk Breakfast Bowl

Lunch: Avocado and Cucumber Sushi Rolls

Dinner: Baked Trout with Dill and Lemon

Dessert: Anti-Inflammatory Turmeric Latte Ice Cream

CONCLUSION

Congratulations on taking a transformative step toward better health with The Simple 5-Ingredient Anti-Inflammatory Cookbook. By embracing simplicity, you've discovered how easy and powerful it can be to heal your body through the food you eat. Each recipe in this book was designed to make healthy eating accessible, flavorful, and, most importantly, sustainable.

Your progress is something to celebrate. Every small change you've made—whether it's swapping processed snacks for wholesome alternatives, preparing quick and nutritious meals, or simply understanding the impact of your food choices—brings you closer to a healthier, more vibrant life. The benefits you're already experiencing, from increased energy to reduced inflammation, are just the beginning.

This journey isn't about perfection but about making consistent, mindful choices that support your health. The simplicity of 5-ingredient recipes proves that nourishing your body doesn't have to be complicated. By focusing on a few high-quality ingredients, you've unlocked the power of real food to reduce inflammation, boost immunity, and improve your overall well-being.

As you move forward, continue to explore and adapt these recipes to fit your lifestyle. Experiment with seasonal ingredients, share your creations with loved ones, and make anti-inflammatory eating a joyful part of your daily routine. This isn't just a diet—it's a foundation for lifelong wellness.

The changes you've embraced will continue to pay off in the long run. Over time, you'll notice improvements in your physical health, mental clarity, and even your emotional well-being. These benefits are a testament to the profound impact of eating with intention and care.

Thank you for letting this cookbook be part of your journey. Remember, the simplest changes often have the most profound effects. May the recipes and principles in this book inspire you to keep prioritizing your health, celebrating your progress, and enjoying every delicious step along the way. Here's to your health and happiness—one bite at a time.

Printed in Great Britain
by Amazon